CIPS Study Matters

Level 5

Advanced Diploma in Purchasing and Supply

PASSNOTES

Improving Supply Chain Performance

Printed and distributed by the Chartered Institute of Purchasing & Supply

Easton House, Easton on the Hill, Stamford, Lincolnshire PE9 3NZ

Tel: +44 (0) 1780 756 777

Fax: +44 (0) 1780 751 610

Email: info@cips.org

Website: www.cips.org

First edition May 2007
Second edition April 2009
Reprinted with minor amendments October 2010

Contents

Preface

Welcome to your **Passnotes**!

This element of your Study Pack has been specially designed to support you in your exam revision.

- Small-format **Passnotes** fit easily into a bag or briefcase: **convenient to use** wherever and whenever you have a few minutes for topic review or exam revision.
- The material is organised in **short, clearly labelled units**: easy to work through systematically or to dip into at any point, if that's what you prefer.
- Each area of the unit content starts with a simple **mind-map** of the relevant Learning Objectives, helpfully **cross-referenced** to chapters in your Course Book (so you can quickly locate more substantial topic coverage, if you need to refresh your memory).
- The units cover each (and all) of the **Learning Objectives** in turn (again, cross-referenced to other units where topics overlap), so you can see exactly what knowledge and understanding underpins potential exam questions.
- Within each unit, the material is presented in a format specially designed for **ease and speed of learning** – essential in the revision stage of your studies! **Passnotes** use key definitions, point lists, action plans, tables and diagrams:
  - To keep the topic coverage as focused and brief as possible
  - To offer an easily grasped overview of each topic
  - To make the topic more visual – and therefore (for most people) more readily memorable.
- For relevant topics, we also include Integrated Learning Checklists: point lists and action plans gathered from different Learning Objectives to give you a broader handle on topics, processes and management challenges. (Particularly useful for case study questions…)

Of course, Passnotes don't give you substantial or comprehensive coverage of the unit content. (That's what your **Course Book** is for.) What they do give you is **systematic and focused coverage**: a concise, easy-to-remember survey of the key points on which you can base an exam answer. This makes them ideal to use in the weeks and days leading up to the exam!

And don't forget: updates, case studies, advice on exam technique and other revision-support resources (including practice questions with full solutions) will be regularly added to the study resources.

Good luck.

Learning Objective 1.0: Developing and improving supplier performance

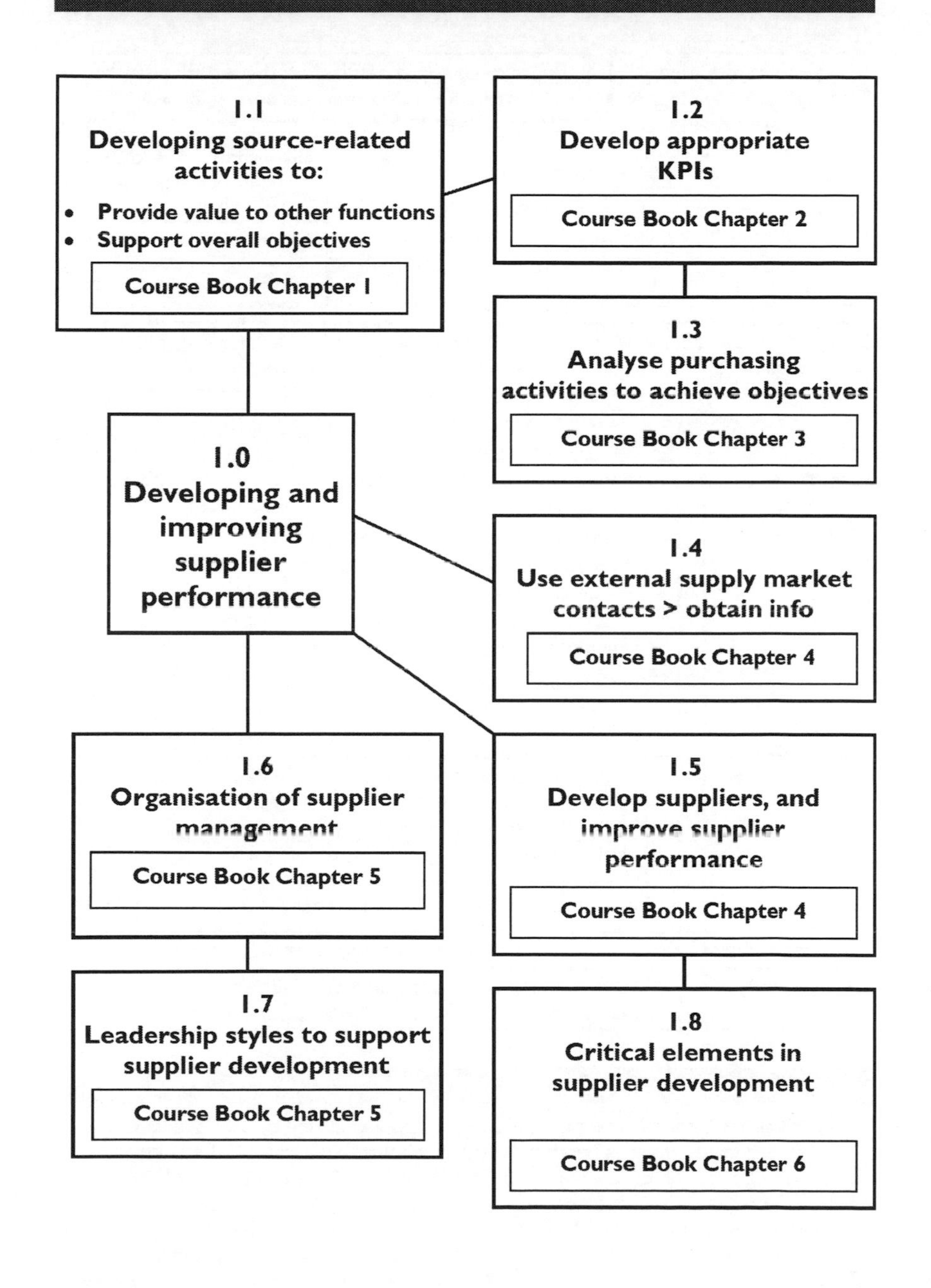

1.1 Develop source-related activities to inform and provide value to other functions and support organisational objectives

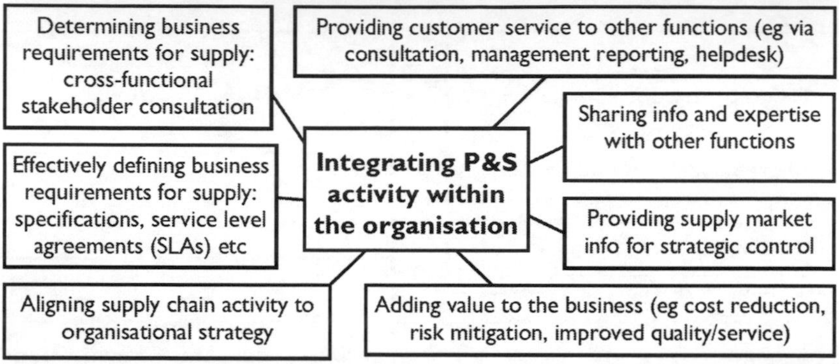

Documenting business requirements

Product/ service specification	Spec communicates **buyer's needs** + establishes **criteria** to judge what is delivered >> buyers need info on **user requirements**: • Design considerations: functionality • Marketing considerations: consumer acceptance • Manufacturing considerations: economical production • Procurement considerations: markets, materials availability, supplier capabilities, cost etc **Effective specification**: up-to-date, detailed technical description, estimate of materials/packaging requirements.
Service level agreements	❑ How often is the service to be provided? ❑ During what hours will the service be carried out? ❑ How many staff will be involved? (> impact on quality) ❑ How far (ie to what specific tasks) will the service extend? ❑ What qualifications are needed by staff? ❑ What speed of response is expected to customer requests? ❑ What procedures will be used to resolve disputes?
Brand/sample	Buyer simply specifies brand name of product required, or supplies sample product for duplication of attributes/functions.

Cross functional teamworking

- ☑ Purchasing > 'internal customer' orientation: communication re user needs/views
- ☑ Increasing involvement of purchasing staff in strategic procurement decisions
- ☑ Increasing adoption of supply chain philosophy > need for integrated work flow
- ☑ Leverages ICT (communication, conferencing, collaborative management tools)
- ☑ World class systems (eg MRP, TQM) require teamwork for implementation
- ☑ Global market/technology development etc > need for diverse expert input
- ☑ Fosters communities of practice (COPs): knowledge sharing, organisational learning

Develop source-related activities to inform and provide value to other functions and support organisational objectives 1.1

☑ Reduction in time to get things done (via co-ordinated effort)
☑ Improved ability to solve complex problems
☑ Improvement in organisation's customer focus
☑ Improved creativity, innovation, learning (via multi-disciplinary interaction)

☒ Managerial challenges: complexity/conflict; ambiguous authority structures; time to develop trust, seek consensus; practical difficulties of meeting, info sharing etc.

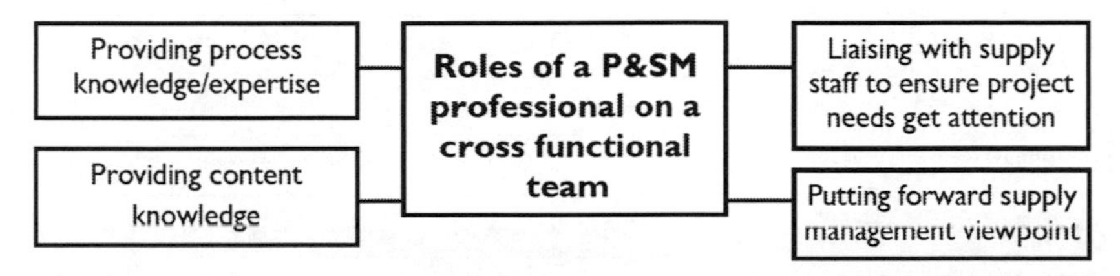

Strategy alignment

Role of purchasing in business/corporate strategy:

- **Implementer**: puts strategy into practice (by achieving five rights)
- **Supporter**: develops policies/procedures/skills needed to reach strategic goals (eg supplier relationships, just in time delivery, cost reduction)
- **Driver:** provides capability to exceed expectations and exploit opportunities (eg through supplier partnership, flexibility)

Corporate objectives	eg Purchasing objectives
Maintain/increase market share	Provide supplies to match customer needs; assure quality; reduce delivery lead time; reduce cost
Improve profit, cash flow	Reduce stocks; improve reliability; more frequent deliveries
Shorten time to market	Early supplier involvement; simultaneous engineering
Reduce non-core activity	Effective make-or-buy policy
Introduce continuous improvement	Reduce supplier base; partnership approaches; reduce product complexity; increase accuracy and reliability

- Potential areas of **conflict** with organisational and/or other functional objectives > agreed **trade-offs** (cost, quality, delivery etc) according to organisational priorities
- Need for **flexibility**/discretion to respond to supply market changes, threats
- Purchasing **performance measures** increasingly integrated with business measures (eg re profitability, quality, corporate social responsibility, ethics)

Interface with the supply market

Purchasing research: ongoing research (and/or defined research projects) into supply markets: to provide info so firm can plan to adapt to changes in supply environment + to secure competitive advantage by early info on opportunities, innovations

1.1 Develop source-related activities to inform and provide value to other functions and support organisational objectives

- ❑ Environmental (PESTLE) factors that may affect continuity or price of supply – eg: scarcity of natural resources; vulnerability to weather/terrorism/industrial action; fluctuating foreign exchange rates affecting prices; new environmental legislation; import quotas and tariffs; consumer values (eg re sustainability, ethical/green issues).
- ❑ Sources of info: supplier/vendor consultation; historical trends; published indices (eg price); economic models; specialist forecasting agencies.

Demand analysis	Vendor analysis	Market analysis
Likely usage of materials in period ahead (> priority focus on high-value, high-usage.)	Performance of potential + current suppliers Optimum type of buying agreement	Structure of market Likely availability/ shortages, prices and price fluctuations of materials

Contribution to added value

- ❑ Cost reduction (eg via price negotiation, global sourcing, purchasing efficiencies, reduced inventory, support for outsourcing etc)
- ❑ Improving supplier performance (eg effective supplier identification, selection, appraisal, performance measurement, contracting and contract management etc)
- ❑ Effective new product development and introduction (eg early purchasing/supplier involvement, purchasing research/info) > reduced costs, improved time-to-market
- ❑ Quality (eg via improved specification, supplier performance management, cross-functional/supply-chain collaboration on continuous improvement)
- ❑ Knowledge management (eg supply market scanning, info-sharing re risks, changes)
- ❑ Waste management (up/down-stream environmental needs and costs; compliance; closed loop supply chains)
- ❑ Risk management (avoidance of unnecessary exposure eg by market intelligence, supplier appraisal, contracting, demand/inventory planning, contingency planning etc)

Internal customer service

- ❑ Awareness of both internal and external customer interfaces: need to build alliances, develop trust, promote/sell ideas, offer added value
- ❑ Requirements for customer relations skills: trust, rapport, empathy with customer needs/problems, positive/collaborative language, seeking feedback, resolving conflict
- ❑ Integrative communication to avoid inter-functional barriers ('silos'): eg cross-functional projects; internal consultancy orientation; 'help-desk' (advisory) service; supportive policies/systems for user-department buyers (eg framework agreements); formal collaborative/consultative structures (eg CLAN, lead buyer)
- ❑ Information sharing with user departments to:
  - Promote P & S's value-adding activities, business case, support for user objectives (> increased influence, status, trust)
  - Add value to user department activity (eg support for product specification, value analysis, quality initiatives)
  - Support managerial planning and control with supply market intelligence

Performance measurement = comparison of current supplier performance against:

- Defined performance criteria or **key performance indicators**
- **Previous performance** (to identify deterioration/improvement trends)
- Other supplier or standard **benchmarks** (to maintain improvement incentive)

Purpose of supplier KPIs

- ❑ To set clear performance criteria/expectations: motivate compliance, improvement
- ❑ To manage supply risk: control quality, delivery, value for money, supply continuity
- ❑ To support contract management: ensuring that agreed benefits are obtained
- ❑ To identify approved/preferred suppliers to support efficient user-department buying
- ❑ To identify suppliers with potential for closer partnership or strategic alliance
- ❑ To support supplier appraisal, improvement, development and reward
- ❑ To provide feedback for learning and continuous improvement (own and supplier)

Developing key performance indicators (KPIs)

Key performance indicators are agreed, quantifiable measures of the performance of a unit or organisation in relation to its critical success factors.

Baseline existing performance — Assess existing performance measures and data collection/reporting methods

↓

Identify critical success factors — Areas of key competitive advantage, or factors necessary for success

↓

Determine measures of success or improvement for each factor/area — Balance quantitative (cost/quantity) & qualitative (subjective/quality) measures

↓

Develop KPIs with key stakeholders — Eg involve users, finance, marketing, suppliers

↓

Agree KPIs with key stakeholders

↓

Communicate KPIs to stakeholders

Ensure KPIs are:

- ☑ Relevant
- ☑ Clear and unambiguous
- ☑ Capable of direct, detailed and consistent measurement at operational level (using available data collection systems)
- ☑ Backed up by incentives/penalties *and* contingency plans (in event of failure)

Supplier KPIs (eg)

Strategic level	Tactical level	Operational level
Lead time v industry norm Quality status/aspirations Cost saving potential Supplier pricing v market Risk management	Efficiency of cycle time Cash flow Quality assurance Capacity flexibility Future growth potential	Delivery performance Quality conformance Responsiveness/agility Technical support

Success factors	Sample KPIs for suppliers
Price	Basic purchase price; profit margin earned by supplier; price compared with other suppliers; cost saving potential
Quality	Reject rates (eg PPM: parts per million non-conformance); adherence to quality standards; frequency of service failure
Delivery	Frequency of late, incorrect or incomplete delivery; proportion of on-time-in-full (OTIF) delivery
Service	Promptness in dealing with enquiries and problems; adherence to agreements on before/after-sales service
Risk/compliance	Ability to meet financial commitments and claims; process capability (ability to repeat conformance reliably); policies and processes compliant with legislation (eg re health and safety, environmental protection, employment ethics)
Overall performance	Benchmarking against other suppliers

Managing compliance with KPIs

Failure by suppliers to meet KPIs leads to:

- ❑ Poor quality inputs > poor quality outputs
- ❑ Costs of disruption, inspection, rejects, complaints adjustment etc + managerial time
- ❑ Knock-on effects eg lost customer goodwill, reputational damage, poor P & S image
- ❑ Unacceptable exposure to supply risk > added costs of risk mitigation: insurances, multiple suppliers, buffer/safety stocks
- ❑ Loss of competitive advantage for supply chain

Managerial controls to support compliance:

- ❑ **Service credits/debits** eg for SLAs for outsourced contracts: buyer claims credits against next period's service fees for shortfalls in service level in current period – but supplier can reduce penalties (via debits) for above-required performance levels.
- ❑ **Incentives:** rewards/awards for compliance/improvement eg: preferred supplier status, increased business, automatic pay-on-receipt, development support.
- ❑ **Gainshare**: sharing of rewards/value gains from improvement eg by flat fee, percentage of profit/savings, use of jointly-developed processes/equipment etc.
- ❑ **Contract terms** providing for fixed sum penalty for breach of contract. If a genuine attempt to estimate/compensate for loss: 'liquidated damages clause' (enforceable). If framed to compel compliance: 'penalty clause' (void: loss/damages decided by court).
- ❑ **Competition:** increased/decreased share of business dependent on compliance
- ❑ **Contract management**: ongoing monitoring and relationship management to ensure contract terms are fulfilled and continuous improvement pursued
- ❑ **Supplier development**: buyer actively supports supplier in fulfilling requirements (eg by training, loan of equipment, info-sharing, performance management)

Benchmarking

Benchmarking is 'the practice of comparing a company's performance against others to stimulate improvements in operating practices'. *(DTI)*

Type	*Focus*
Competitive	Comparing the organisation's performance with industry competitors.
Functional/ generic	Comparing similar processes/functions across industries > continuous improvement and demonstrable competitive edge.
Performance	Comparing performance measures (eg CAPS indices for purchasing and supplier performance)
Process	Comparing the performance/functionality of a process against 'best practice' exponents of that process

☑ Learning from the successes (and mistakes) of others > confidence, flexibility
☑ Stretching KPIs (+ competitive advantage) through matching competitor performance
☑ Enhances supplier motivation through competitive element
☑ Increased improvement-focused communication and collaboration

Supplier appraisal and selection

☑ Manage supply risk: ongoing control of sources of strategic/critical items
☑ Identify/qualify new sources for strategic/critical items
☑ Identify/select sources of new or one-off products/services

Criteria for assessing supplier desirability/capability

Lysons & Farrington	*Ten Cs*	*FACE 2 FACE*
Adequacy and care of production equipment	Competence	Fixed assets
Personal attitudes	Capacity	Ability to deliver
Means of controlling quality	Costs	Cost
Housekeeping	Commitment (to quality)	Efficiency
Competence: technical staff	Control (of processes)	
Competence: management	Cash (financial stability)	Financial stability
	Consistency (of output)	Ability to work w. buyer
	Cultural compatibility	Commitment to quality
	Clean (environmentally)	Environmental factors
	Compliance (or CSR)	

Supplier auditing (on-site visits or capability surveys)

☑ Important source of info (by questionnaire, observation and on-site interviews) on:

- Production equipment, operations and capacity
- Operation of key materials management activities
- Expertise and motivation of personnel
- Technological know-how of supervisors and management capabilities

☒ Costly, time-consuming approach: reserve for strategic items, short-listed suppliers

Supplier evaluation

- **Numerical/statistical** – eg vendor rating, financial ratios
- **Perception based** – eg Carter's 10Cs, stakeholder feedback, supplier SWOT
- **Research based** – eg financial accounts, customer references
- **Accreditation based** – eg ISO 9001:2000; SERVQUAL service benchmarks
- **Self-assessment based** – eg supplier reports, audits

❑ Monitor performance according to agreed KPIs etc **[>> *Unit 1.2*]**
❑ Contract management: ensure contract terms performed
❑ Relationship management: develop communication, trust, continuous improvement

Purchasing contribution to quality

Total quality management (TQM) is an orientation to quality in which quality values and aspirations are applied to the management of *all* resources and relationships within the firm and throughout the value chain, in order to seek continuous improvement and excellence in all aspects of performance.

Manage purchasing activities to influence the ability of the organisation to achieve its objectives — 1.3

Customer	Quality is defined by customer satisfaction (or delight)
Get it right first time	Quality can leverage or lose custom; costs of prevention less than cost of correction > goal of zero defects/errors
Continuous improvement	*Kaizen* (continuous incremental improvement) approach empowers staff > creativity, problem-solving, quality thinking
Process alignment	Processes designed and modified so every activity is geared to same end: meeting customer needs/wants.
Total involvement	Cross-functional team-based management (eg quality circles) > collaboration, communication, breaking down of 'silos'.
Quality chains	From suppliers to ultimate consumers
Win-win relationships	Supply chain relationships based on recognition of strategic importance > mutually beneficial, long-term relationship.

Purchasing contribution via:

- ❑ Product development: early involvement; value engineering; materials specification
- ❑ Supplier selection and appraisal: eg approved supplier lists, certification
- ❑ Contract management eg mutual understanding of standards, incentives/penalties etc
- ❑ Monitoring and managing quality and timely delivery of incoming supplies
- ❑ Supplier relations > collaborative quality management, continuous improvement
- ❑ Measurement, evaluation and improvement of supplier performance eg vendor rating
- ❑ Support for cross-functional teamworking and involvement
- ❑ Orientation to management across the supply/value/quality chain

Process improvement models

- ☑ Horizontal (process) focus > remove vertical barriers to work/info/value flow
- ☑ Management of interfaces/linkages in supply chain to secure added value
- ☑ Integrated systems > flexible response to complex inputs, change in global markets
- ☑ Cost improvements > potential for gain sharing (rather than supplier margin erosion)

Control charts	Sample outputs inspected when process working well, to establish 'control limits' (boundaries of acceptable output) > seek/rectify causes of subsequent unacceptable variation.
PDCA and DMAIC	Structured frameworks for continuous improvement: • Plan, Do, Check, Act. • Define (the problem); Measure (performance); Analyse (causes); Improve (the process); Control.
Six Sigma	Application of statistical problem solving tools to identify/quantify quality problems and indicate steps for improvement. • Focus on characteristics critical to quality for customers • Design/improve/manage processes to reduce defects • Work cross-functionally ('boundaryless collaboration')
Kaizen	Continuous, small-step, bottom-up incremental improvements
Value analysis	Systematic study of materials/systems to identify potential to eliminate unnecessary cost or waste without losing value.
Quality function deployment	Multi-functional teams translate customer needs into technical specs for each stage of activity along the supply chain.

Purchasing planning

- Planning and control > purchasing discipline, efficiency, effectiveness:

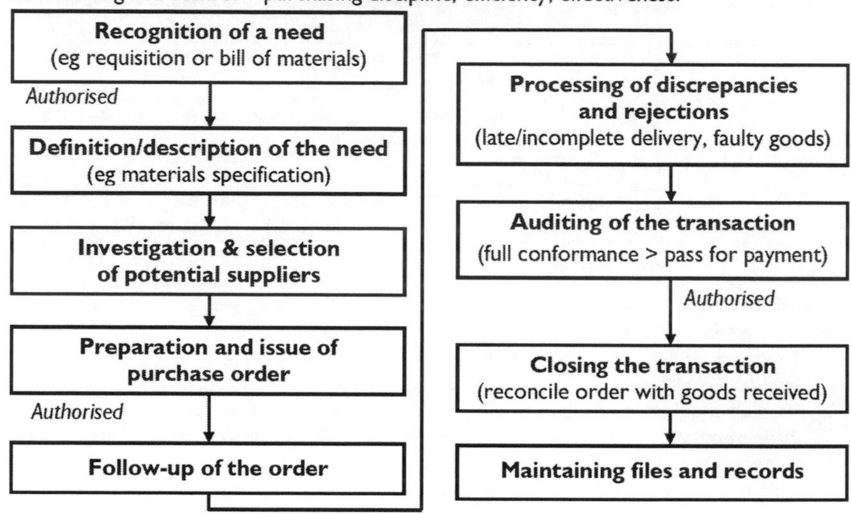

- Contribution to **fiscal planning**: supplying accurate materials cost forecasts; alternative sourcing strategies; own budgetary control and compliance.

- Contribution to **research & development (R & D)**: identifying third-party alliances; supplier selection; materials specification; mediating early supplier involvement and/or co-engineering; ongoing cross-functional development activity.

Vendor rating

Quantitative measures of price, quality and delivery aspects of supplier performance.

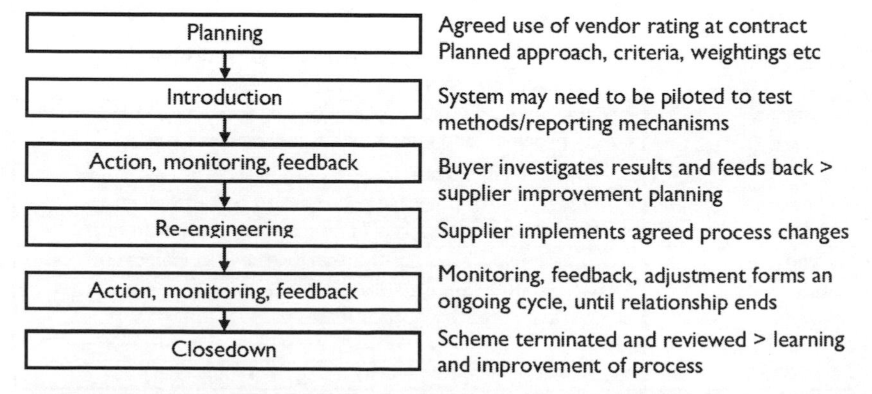

(Checklist and factor rating methods: *see Chapter 2 of your Course Book*)

1.4 Evaluate and explain the importance of external contacts with the supply market

Innovation is 'the successful exploitation of new ideas' (*DTI*). In supply market terms, it is about exploiting new technologies and their applications by suppliers to deliver more effective and efficient products/services.

- ❑ New products/processes for previously unmet market needs (eg via market research)
- ❑ New products/processes for existing market needs (new technology – eg RFID, e-commerce – or knowledge/intellectual property: eg new design, consultancy services)
- ❑ Use of existing products/services/processes in new applications (eg outsourcing)
- ❑ Incremental improvements to existing products/processes (eg *kaizen*, six sigma)

Supply market research is the process of gathering, analysing and evaluating supply data to identify business opportunities, risks and threats.

- ❑ Structure of the supply market (number of buyers/suppliers, competition, power etc)
- ❑ Likely availability/shortages, prices/price fluctuations of materials
- ❑ Methods of pricing used; degree of product differentiation etc
- ❑ New materials, products/services and processes emerging in the market
- ❑ Environmental factors that may affect continuity or price of supply – eg: scarcity of natural resources; vulnerability to weather/terrorism/industrial action; legislation; consumer values (eg re ethical/green issues); new technology developments

Supplier analysis is a micro-level analysis of the capabilities of individual suppliers within the market.

- ❑ Supplier background, development, track record
- ❑ Capacity and process capability
- ❑ Identified strengths and weaknesses ***[>> also Unit 1.3]***
- ❑ Cost analysis
- ❑ Quality assurance (and other compliance) systems

Market intelligence is the product of ongoing gathering, analysis and evaluation of market data to support strategic and tactical decision-making. It includes **competitive intelligence**, which refers specifically to information about direct and indirect competitors.

Reverse engineering is a technique for learning about/from competitor products/services by micro-analysing their make up.

- ❑ Identify how product works + weaknesses in quality or functionality >> ideas for improvement/competition, analysis of competitor costs etc.
- ❑ NB: potential ethical/legal issues: may strengthen complaint of breach of patent/©.

Intel sources

- Contacts, networking, conferences etc
- Published economic/industry models and indices
- Suppliers, vendors, distributors, customers
- Published statistical reports and benchmark standards
- Observation, sampling etc of processes/products
- Third-party researchers, analysts and consultants

Evaluate and explain the importance of external contacts with the supply market 1.4

Supply market research process *(van Weele)*

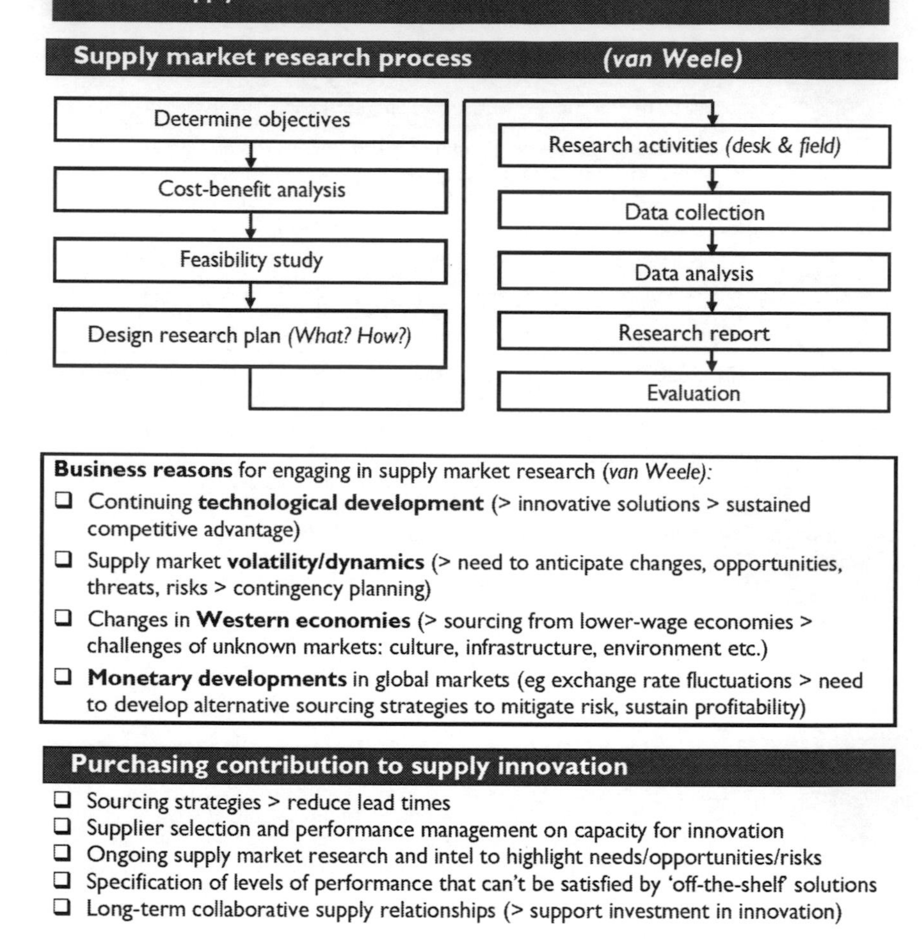

Business reasons for engaging in supply market research *(van Weele):*

- ❑ Continuing **technological development** (> innovative solutions > sustained competitive advantage)
- ❑ Supply market **volatility/dynamics** (> need to anticipate changes, opportunities, threats, risks > contingency planning)
- ❑ Changes in **Western economies** (> sourcing from lower-wage economies > challenges of unknown markets: culture, infrastructure, environment etc.)
- ❑ **Monetary developments** in global markets (eg exchange rate fluctuations > need to develop alternative sourcing strategies to mitigate risk, sustain profitability)

Purchasing contribution to supply innovation

- ❑ Sourcing strategies > reduce lead times
- ❑ Supplier selection and performance management on capacity for innovation
- ❑ Ongoing supply market research and intel to highlight needs/opportunities/risks
- ❑ Specification of levels of performance that can't be satisfied by 'off-the-shelf' solutions
- ❑ Long-term collaborative supply relationships (> support investment in innovation)

Testing and evaluating supply innovations: ***[>> also Unit 1.5, 1.8]***

- ❑ Systematic supply market/competitor research and intel
- ❑ Detailed feasibility study, risk assessment, cost/benefit analysis
- ❑ Benchmarking products/processes (and/or innovation indicators)
- ❑ Pre-testing of new products/processes (eg prototyping, test/phased implementation)
- ❑ Innovation KPIs eg: R & D investment, education/training spend, patent registrations, technical papers/articles; new products/processes introduced

Purchasing contribution to business forecasting

- ❑ Inputs: intelligence relating to market trends, influencing factors, risks, materials costs
- ❑ Interface with supply networks > intelligence for refining projections
- ❑ Cross-functional awareness/consultation > info-sharing for integrated forecasts
- ❑ Overview of (and contacts with) supply chain > understanding of financial risk issues, cost structures, demand forecasting techniques etc.

Propose ways to develop new and existing suppliers and improve their performance 1.5

Identifying and appraising new suppliers *[>> Unit 1.3]*

- *Low-value, non-critical items:* desk-based research into supplier quality/delivery performance (eg transaction history) or capability (eg customer references, samples)
- *More important items:* classify suppliers from which user departments can order without further checking eg as approved supplier (satisfies basic technical/quality criteria) or preferred supplier (track record of satisfactory performance)
- *Critical items:* more rigorous measurement required before contract award: eg site visits, external supplier accreditation (eg ISO 9000 quality assurance).

Evaluating and improving existing supplier performance

- Performance measurement and management
- Vendor rating *[>> Unit 1.3]*
- Contract and relationship management *[>> Unit 2.1]*
- Supplier development *[>> Unit 1.8]*

Value analysis, management and engineering

Value analysis is 'the organised, systematic study of the function of a material, part, component or system to identify areas of unnecessary cost.' *(Zenz)* **Value engineering** is the application of VA from the development stage onwards.

Tests for value

- Does the use of the material, part or process contribute value?
- Is the cost of the material, part or process proportionate to its usefulness?
- Are all the product features actually needed?
- Can a lower-cost method be used – *while* retaining the features and functions that add value?
- Is anyone paying less for this part?

Analysis covers: **S**tandardisation; **T**ransport classification; **O**ver-engineering; **P**ackaging; **S**ubstitute materials; **W**eight; **A**ny unnecessary processing; **S**upplier input; **T**o make (v buy); **E**liminate (waste, obsolescence, redundancy) **>> "STOPS WASTE"**

- ☑ Ensure quality built in at design stage: reduce need for engineering changes later
- ☑ Reduce time to market
- ☑ Reduce development/production costs
- ☑ Improve cross-functional collaboration on responsiveness to customer needs

Value management (VM) evolved out of value analysis to focus on the effectiveness and efficiency of other business resources. It has come to describe a management style focused on motivating people, developing skills and promoting innovation, in order to optimise overall organisation performance.

- ☑ Improved provision of products/services through focus on customer, value
- ☑ Enhanced competitiveness through innovation, flexibility, organisational learning
- ☑ Unity of direction through common value culture, improved internal communication
- ☑ Enhanced co-ordination and efficiency through cross-functional teamworking

Collaboration on performance improvement

- Competition between supply chains (not just organisations) > suppliers regarded as extension of the enterprise (especially where services/operations outsourced)
- Collaborative supply relationships: buyer seeks to develop long-term, mutually beneficial relationship with suppliers. Proactive joint search for improvements, innovations > sharing value gains.
- Joint quality initiatives: eg shared training, accreditation, *kaizen* or six sigma programmes; supplier expertise > product development and materials specification
- Joint efficiency/cost initiatives: eg sharing of cost data, joint waste reduction schemes, value analysis/engineering, collaborative forward planning, integrated systems/processes for reduced transaction costs (eg EDI), consignment stock or vendor managed inventory facilities etc.

Purchasing contribution:

- ❑ Establishment and development of relationships
- ❑ Supplier motivation (performance management, incentives, gainsharing etc)
- ❑ Development of shared performance measures (focus on mutual benefits)
- ❑ Support (business case) for supply chain management orientation to competitiveness

Supply switching

Reasons for switching suppliers:

- ❑ Problems with existing supplier performance
- ❑ New supplier offers better bid for new contract period
- ❑ New supplier can capitalise on opportunities (eg new technology) better
- ❑ Low-risk items, transactional relationship > ease of opportunistic switching

Risks of changing supplier
New supplier may fail to perform (eg exaggerated claims to win contract…)
Process incompatibility (eg if specific modifications made for old supplier)
Cultural/inter-personal incompatibility
Loss of knowledge (eg where collaborative processes undocumented)
Learning curve: time to achieve peak performance, teething problems
Exposure to unfamiliar supply risks
Exposure of intellectual property, data

Costs of changing supplier
Identifying/qualifying new suppliers: search, appraisal etc.
Initiating/administering tendering exercise (mandatory in the public sector)
Not-yet-delivered items; outstanding claims
Change of systems and processes to align with new supplier (plus training etc)
Exit fees (contractual obligations to old supplier eg for early cancellation)
Contract development and management
Risk mitigation measures (eg insurance)

- ❑ **Switching costs** are costs incurred as a result of switching.
- ❑ **Sunk costs** are costs already incurred with the current supplier (eg investments in equipment, modifications, R & D): cannot be recovered on switching

Propose ways to develop new and existing suppliers and improve their performance 1.5

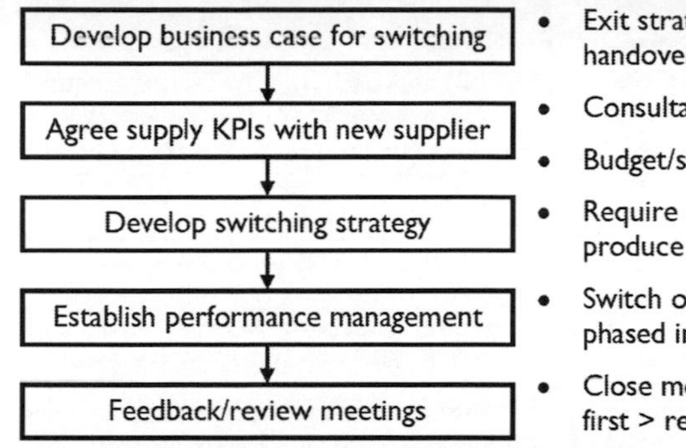

- Exit strategy for contract transition (eg handover clauses, protection of IP etc)
- Consultation with users/stakeholders
- Budget/share risks/costs of switching
- Require old and new suppliers to produce smooth transition plans
- Switch over tactics (ramp-up/ramp-down, phased implementation, parallel supply)
- Close monitoring and frequent review at first > reduce as confidence increases

Managing supply innovation

- **Incremental supply innovation** (improvement of existing supply systems) often managed by trialling or piloting the concept within clearly defined areas of the business; parallel/phased implementation etc.
- **Phase-gate process**. Defined deliverables or success criteria for each phase must be 'passed' before authorised to proceed to next stage. Business risk assessment > stakeholder communication > establish pilot area > establish KPIs > implement pilot > evaluate pilot > proceed decision > develop company-wide rollout plan.
- **Radical supply innovation** (exploration of new supply concepts eg e-procurement) often managed by more complex company-wide project management techniques (engagement of sponsors, stakeholder management, external consultancy etc)

Managing supply risk

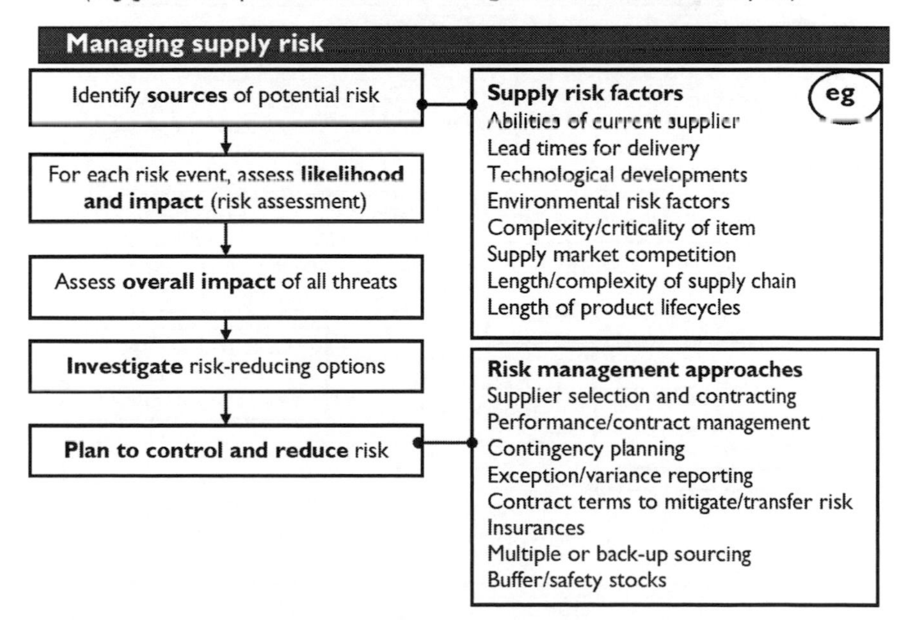

1.6 Devise appropriate supplier management organisational models and demonstrate how other functions might interact in these models

Supplier management organisation models

In a **Single Point of Contact (SPOC)** approach, the purchasing function is the sole communication interface (or 'gatekeeper') for dealings with the supplier. Alternatively, **multiple contact (or 'touch') points** may be used.

Single point of contact	v	**Multiple touch points**
Can be effective in relatively small, centralised operations.		Often used in larger, more complex operations.
Difficulties increase with complexity of markets, organisations and products		Procurement role > facilitator in managing multiple relationships across the firm
Does not support SCM orientation: supplier/buyer pairing is only one link in the value chain, tiered supply etc.		Supported by integrated info systems > coherent, co-ordinated multi-touch interface
Point of contact may be procurement function buyer or user buyer		Touch points: procurement, finance, engineering, user buyers, business review meetings, supply project teams etc

Benefits:	***Benefits:***
Consistent, coherent communication	Diverse inputs to relationship/solutions
Experience of 'one-stop' service	Supports direct stakeholder involvement
Development of relationship over time	Avoids interface 'bottlenecks'
Avoids risk of divergent info/needs	Increased supplier flexibility/options
Encourages 'ownership' of relationship	Reduces bias, personal incompatibility
Efficiency (less redundancy, repetition)	Increased supply chain responsiveness

Interface	v	**Integration**
Interactions or transactions: firms 'touch' at their boundaries, often by single contact points.		Firms 'overlap' boundaries: shared process/info systems (eg EDI, internet, extranet); planning co-ordination and resource sharing; communication links (often at multiple points of contact); joint strategy and performance measures.

Roles in supplier management and development

Relationship management

- Early supplier involvement: joint development/clarification of requirement and performance measures
- Collaboration in management and problem solving (supplier in difficulties)
- Constructive dispute resolution (eg by conciliation/arbitration)
- Supplier motivation: contract incentives/penalties; recognition systems
- Contract management: performance monitoring, change co-ordinating, review/feedback
- Supplier feedback, development and training (eg in statistical process control, JIT, TQM)
- Managing relationship growth and decline

Devise appropriate supplier management organisational models and demonstrate how other functions might interact in these models 1.6

- ❑ **Purchasing function** acts as facilitator of relationship, depending on role and structure in the organisation: administrative (eg transaction processing), commercial (eg contract development and management) or strategic (eg supply chain development, collaboration in added value strategies).
- ❑ **Cross-functional sourcing team**: personnel from at least three functions brought together to complete a purchasing/materials management initiative (*Trent & Monczka)*.
  - What relationships justify cost of cross-functional management? eg strategic items (Kraljic matrix), or desire to be 'core' customer (supplier preferencing)
  - Benefits for supply relationships:
    - ☑ Improved communication re performance improvement, stakeholder needs
    - ☑ Improved internal integration of purchasing objectives and systems
    - ☑ Foundation for supplier integration (eg in NPD, integrated info systems)
    - ☑ Shared performance measures linked to business objectives
- ❑ **Executive sponsor(s):** senior executive (ideally in both organisations) with overall responsibility for relationship management and development.
  - Ensure alignment of strategic objectives with supplier development objectives
  - Co-ordinate multiple touch points > consistency, coherence
  - Actively promote the relational alliance concept
  - Monitor collaborative value-adding initiatives
  - Manage conflicts which can't be resolved by core teams
  - Open dialogue on mutual business issues and future opportunities

Decentralised purchasing functions

Advantages of centralisation		**Advantages of decentralisation**
Specialisation of purchasing staff		Max communication/co-ordination between purchasing and operating units
Consolidation of requirements (eg consortia) > economies of scale		Quicker response to user/customer needs
Co-ordination: standard policies/ procedures, approved suppliers etc		Relationship with local suppliers > shorter supply lines, sustainability (public sector)
Less conflict between buying units	↓	Smaller quantities > reduced inventory cost
Skill/resource for purchasing research		Managerial accountability for performance

Part-centralised, part local *(Lysons)* or **hybrid**.

- ❑ **Centre-led action network (CLAN):** procurement staff located in business units (*decentralised*). Report primarily to local management, with secondary responsibility to head-office procurement centre (*matrix*) which leads/co-ordinates network; sets standards; encourages best practice (*centre-led*) >> co-ordinated decentralisation
- ❑ **Lead buyer:** delegation of defined responsibilities for category purchases > individual within a user dept. or business unit (usually with the highest requirement for that category) > creation of 'virtual' category teams, led by lead buyers.
  - ☑ User departments/units closely involved in purchasing decisions
  - ☑ Centralised purchasing > consolidated orders, leverage, expertise etc.
  - ☒ Lead buyer not a procurement professional > needs support from purchasing staff

1.7 Describe appropriate leadership styles to support supplier development

Supplier development

Supplier development is the process whereby a buying organisation assists a supplier to fulfil its requirements.

- Enhancing working relationships (eg by improved communication systems, routines)
- Increasing performance goals (eg by reducing waste and speeding up delivery)
- Requiring supplier capability improvements (eg in quality or communications)
- Providing support personnel, training or information to support improvements
- Providing capital or equipment ***[>> Unit 1.8]***

Influencing suppliers (eg to improve performance)

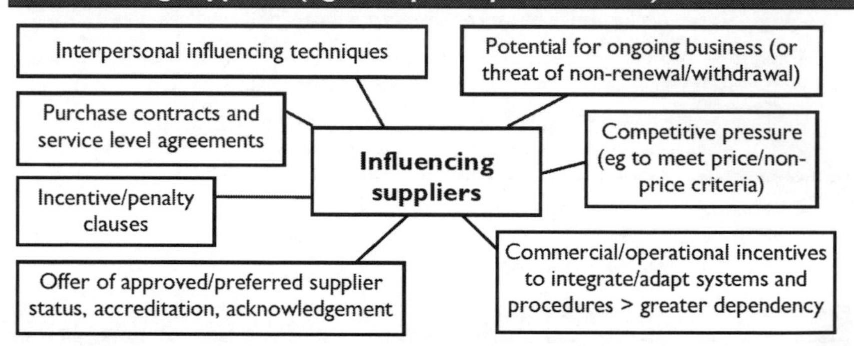

Incentives to develop and improve

- **Supplier awards** eg for quality, service, price, cost reduction, CSR. (NB aligned with performance objectives, cost/benefit analysed and with tangible value.)
- **Preferred supplier status** (or equivalent > competitive advantage)
- **Potential for future business** (especially if benefiting from guaranteed volume)
- **Gainsharing**: a negotiated approach to sharing financial benefits of value gains (or cost reductions) with suppliers responsible for them. Contract clause allows the supplier to retain a defined portion of any successful cost reduction initiative.
  - ☑ Incentive to measurable financial performance improvements
  - ☑ Generates a win-win culture and improved relational/improvement interface
  - ☑ Flexibility: suited to each particular contract
  - ☑ Creates opportunity and rationale for greater supplier involvement
  - ☒ Costs of agreement, monitoring, measurement, management
  - ☒ Requires transparency and ease of measurement from business systems
  - ☒ Requires a high level of mutual trust
  - ☒ If inflexible, environmental changes (eg commodity prices) may cause frustration

Describe appropriate leadership styles to support supplier development 1.7

Performance measures and supplier development

- Provide direction for development: clarify buyer expectations and needs
- Stimulate feedback on performance, focus for information-gathering and problem-solving, highlight areas for improvement/development planning
- Motivation for development (especially if tied to positive incentives: less effective to 'name and shame' under-performing suppliers)
- Basis for rationalisation of supply base > support selected supplier development
- Shared performance measures > collaborative approach, mutual benefit
- Balanced quality/time/cost objectives > encourage flexible added value thinking
- Need for consistency > opportunity for development over time

Leadership styles to support supplier development

Hersey & Blanchard: situational leadership

Most appropriate style depends on follower (supplier/stakeholder) readiness/maturity.

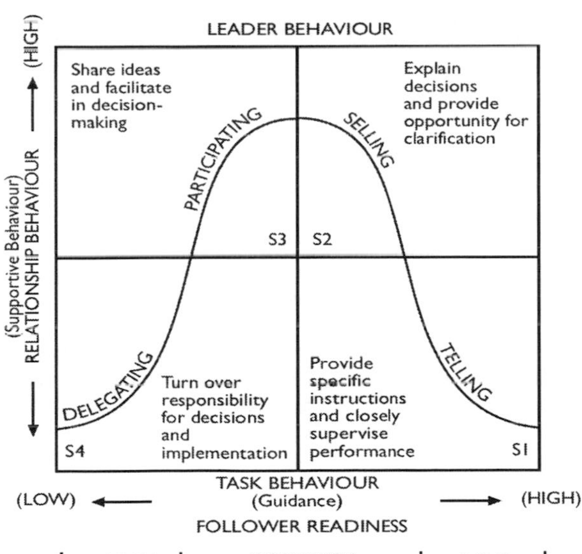

HIGH	MODERATE		LOW
R4	R3	R2	R1
Able and Willing or Confident	Able but Unwilling or Insecure	Unable but Willing or Confident	Unable and Unwilling or Insecure

FOLLOWER DIRECTED (R4–R3) — LEADER DIRECTED (R2–R1)

Selling: *ensures that expectations are understood; allows for stakeholder/supplier input; fosters involvement/flexibility – but retains control.*

Telling: *ensures control (eg if results critical or supplier new) – but does not encourage input, dialogue, development, initiative in problem-solving.*

1.8 Identify the critical elements of supplier development

Requirements for successful supplier development

- ❑ Clear business case and cost/benefit analysis *(See next page)*
- ❑ Prioritisation of suppliers/relationships for development ***[>> Unit 2.1]***
- ❑ Collaborative teamworking environment ***[Unit 1.1, 1.6, 1.7]***
- ❑ Clear KPIs and systematic performance measurement ***[>> Unit 1.3, 1.5, 1.7, 2.4]***
- ❑ Appropriate incentives (including gainsharing) ***[>> Unit 1.7]***

Joint problem-solving with suppliers

- ❑ Collaborative approach and purchasing contribution ***[>> Unit 1.5]***
- ❑ Internal/cross-functional communication requirements ***[>> Unit 1.7]***
- ❑ Benefits of collaborative (rather than competitive) approaches
- ❑ **Structural mechanisms**: joint quality circles, project teams or task forces; communities of practice (COPs); ongoing contacts; rotating staff visits/secondments.

☑ Establish mutual norms and expectations
☑ Develop interpersonal contacts and collaborative relationships
☑ Leverage supplier expertise > added value, innovation
☑ Encourage early info exchange (eg early supplier involvement)
☑ Mitigate and/or share risks

Continuous improvement

Kaizen is the Japanese term for continuous improvement. 'It is both a rigorous, scientific method of using statistical quality control and an adaptive framework of organisational values and beliefs that keep management and workers alike focused on zero defects'.

- **Kaizen**: continuous improvement by incremental (small step) improvements.

Plan	Implement (small scale)	Measure	Evaluate results/process > identify learning

- **Hansei kaizen:** continuous improvement through rigorous self-reflection: constant monitoring, questioning and feedback-seeking > open to areas for improvement.
- **Kaizen teian** ('proposal'): involving all employees as collaborators in continuous improvement: eg cross-functional kaizen teams work together to plan and implement incremental improvement projects.
- **Quality circles (QCs):** small groups of employees from all levels/functions meet with facilitator to discuss quality issues and (depending on terms of reference) make recommendations or prepare action plans. Company-wide QC activities driven by steering committee, administered by co-ordinator. Delegates may be trained eg in quality control, operating procedures, teamworking and problem-solving.

☑ Employees become 'process owners' > commitment to continuous improvement
☑ Developing skills in quality, team processes, problem-solving, leadership
☑ Breaking down functional and hierarchical barriers to teamworking
☑ Measurable quality/process improvements

Process improvement techniques

- ❑ Process improvement techniques (including six sigma) *[>> Unit 1.3]*
- ❑ Business process re-engineering (BPR) *[>> Unit 2.5]*

Six Sigma is an application of statistical problem-solving tools to identify and quantify quality problems and indicate steps for improvement.

Process improvement	**DMAIC**: Define (problem), Measure (performance of process), Analyse (causes of defects), Improve, Control.
Process (re-) design	**DMADV**: Define (goals for new process); Match/measure (performance measures); Analyse (process requirements); Design (and implement process); Verify (that goals are being met).
Process management	Monitor customer requirements, environmental changes; measure performance against KPIs; refine KPIs; control process performance by responding to variations (outside tolerances).

Developing supplier innovation

- ❑ Developing, testing and evaluating innovation *[>> Unit 1.4, 1.5]*
- ❑ **Innovation council**: small, cross-functional team of senior managers that co-ordinate and direct innovation management activities across all business functions:
  - Formulation of innovation strategies
  - Development of innovation KPIs and metrics
  - Co-ordination of innovation processes across units/functions
  - Development of evaluation/reward mechanisms
- ❑ **Breakthrough value creation** (discontinuous innovation): transformation of product/process for significant value gains (v 'continuous/incremental' improvement). Eg e-procurement, RFID tracking, move to JIT, supply chain agility, global sourcing.

Evaluating supplier development

Buyer's perspective	*Supplier's perspective*
☑ Support outsourcing strategy ☑ Improving time-to-market, quality, delivery or price > increased sales and profitability ☑ Streamlining systems for process efficiencies, cost savings ☑ Gaining discounts or other benefits as a *quid pro quo* for development	☑ Production and process efficiencies, cost savings > profitability ☑ Improvement in customer satisfaction > retained/increased business ☑ Improved capacity, service levels > additional sales to other customers ☑ Direct gains in knowledge, resources, ☑ Enhanced learning, flexibility
☒ Managerial costs in identifying and negotiating opportunities ☒ Cost of activities and resources: risk of over-investment ☒ Risk of sharing intellectual property	☒ Managerial costs ☒ Investment in systems/infra-structure ☒ Cost of discounts or exclusivity agreements given as *quid pro quo* ☒ Risks of over-dependence

Learning Objective 2.0: Maximising competitiveness

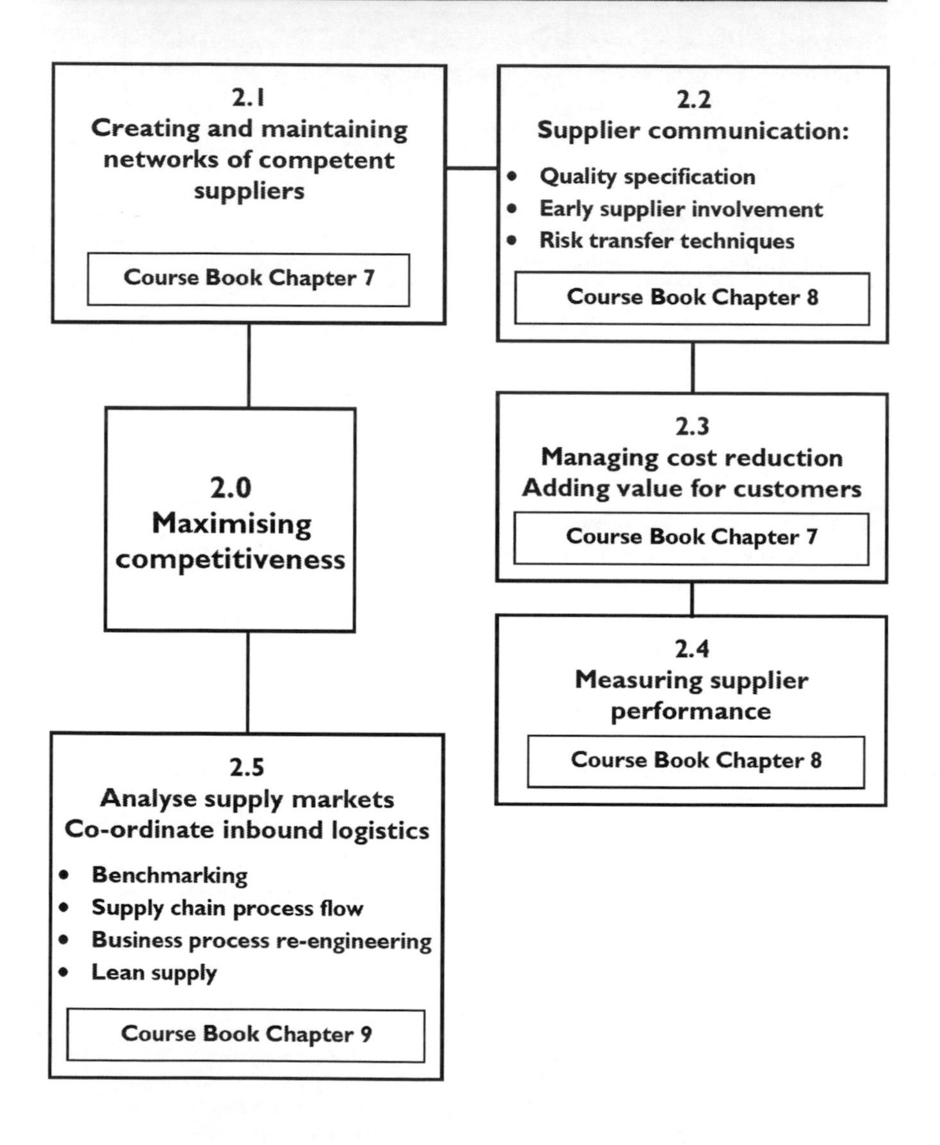

Manage systematic efforts to create and maintain networks of competent suppliers and to develop their capabilities — 2.1

Supplier segmentation

Supplier segmentation is the categorisation of suppliers according to their 'importance', in order to prioritise purchasing resource and determine the relational approach that will best balance cost efficiency and risk management.

Pareto (ABC) analysis

>> *Categorise on basis of value and volume of business with each supplier*

Pareto principle (80:20 rule) > categorise stock items: small number, high usage/value (Category A: 'vital few'); medium number/usage/value (Category B: 'normal'); high number, low usage/value (Category C: 'trivial many').

- Prioritise investment in alliance/development > small number of Category A suppliers
- Category B/C: 'low maintenance' replenishment (eg vendor managed inventory)

Kraljic matrix (supply positioning model)

>> *Categorise on basis of importance to the organisation of the item being purchased, and supply risk (danger that product may be unavailable when needed).*

- ***Non-critical:*** KPI = functional efficiency.
- ***Leverage:*** KPI = cost/price, materials flow management.
- ***Bottleneck:*** KPI = cost management, reliable short-term sourcing.
- ***Strategic:*** KPI = long term supply continuity.

Complexity of the supply market

Importance of item to the organisation	*Low*	*High*
Low	**Routine or non-critical items** Require systems contract approach to purchasing	**Bottleneck items** Require continuity of supply
High	**Leverage items** Require competitive bidding	**Strategic items** Require a 'partnership and alliance' approach

Supplier preferencing (PMMS model)

>> *Categorise* buyers *on basis of attractiveness to suppliers.*

Buyer attractiveness factors eg:

Glamour or high profile
Reputation (eg CSR)
Fair dealing, prompt payment
Info-sharing, collaboration
Financial viability, success
Future plans

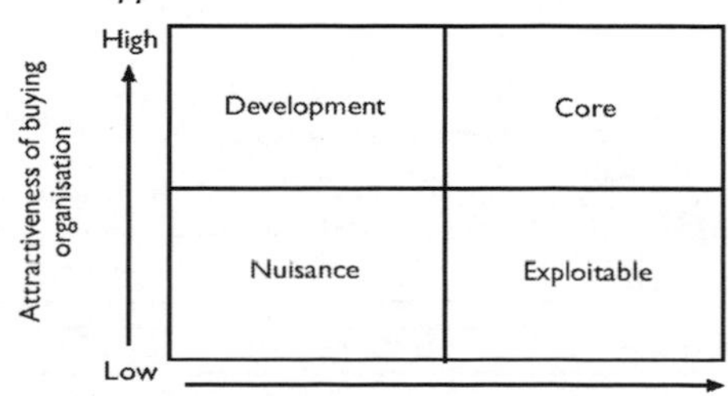

NB: transactional/competitive relationships, buyer has no need to be 'attractive', but for strategic supplies > attention to developing/maintaining 'good customer' status.

2.1 Manage systematic efforts to create and maintain networks of competent suppliers and to develop their capabilities

Supplier tiering

Tier 1: strategic, high value-added, high risk, innovative
Tier 2: regular purchases, medium-high value, framework agreements
Tier 3: commodity items, one-off purchases, little relationship or value added.

(NB term also used for multi-level supply chain structure*: see your Course Book.)*

Supplier management

Supplier segmentation	• Define relative supplier importance (using appropriate models) • Determine appropriate resources/tactics for categories
Internal coordination	• Agree methods and standards for buyer-supplier interface • Coordinate supplier inputs, flow through internal supply chains.
Supplier performance management	• Develop supplier KPIs, incentives, info interfaces and flows, support mechanisms, monitoring/review mechanisms etc to control supplier performance on an ongoing basis.
Supplier partnership	• Select compatible/capable suppliers of strategic items > prioritise partnership resources (NB: compatibility of 'clockspeed' *[Fine]:* pace of change/adaptation) • Develop collaborative initiatives to optimise business returns • Coordinate internal and external partnership activities • Develop tools and incentives for meaningful info-sharing • Focus on mutual benefits and sharing of value gains

What sort of relationship?

- Importance of item being purchased (critical items > closer relationship)
- Capability of supplier (low capability: no benefit in partnership)
- Supply market conditions (fast change, high competition > increased risk in partnership)
- Geographical location (distant > more difficult partnership, despite ICT)

Supplier rationalisation

Supplier rationalisation (supply-base reduction, supplier consolidation) is the process of optimising the number of suppliers used by an organisation.

Stage	**Supply base** *(Treasury Central Unit on Procurement)*
Innocence	Large number of suppliers, selected at random
Awareness	Large number of suppliers, but most spend > only a few
Understanding	Reduced number of selected suppliers > benefits of closer relationship
Competence	Partnership with suppliers for key items + multi-sourcing for non-key
Excellence	Ongoing programme to optimise supply base > strategic objectives

Reduced number of suppliers:

- ☑ Focused use of procurement resources and buyer time
- ☑ Reduced selection/appraisal, transaction and purchase costs (eg volume discounts)
- ☑ Selection of higher-capability suppliers (process capability, innovation, synergy)
- ☑ Closer, stable relationships > investment in cost reduction, quality programmes, innovation, integration (eg e-procurement)
- ☑ Rewards high-performing suppliers > motivate continuous improvement
- ☒ Erosion of supplier competition (> multi-source for non-key items to secure competitive pricing; avoid complacency with innovation/improvement KPIs etc)
- ☒ Increased dependency > risk of exposure (> back-up sources for strategic items)
- ☒ Increased transparency > risk of exposure (> protect intellectual property etc)
- ☒ Costs of gaining internal consensus, specifying supply base design, developing partnership management (> prioritise resources on strategic relationships)

A framework for supplier rationalisation	
Stakeholder consultation	Communicate intentions to internal stakeholders: gather info re needs, established supplier relationships, risk assessment etc.
Supplier segmentation	Identify key/strategic purchases and/or suppliers (using appropriate models)
Establish qualification criteria	Develop clear business retention criteria and performance qualifiers. (Ideally, determined by multi-functional stakeholder team.) Eg criteria re volume (eg contracts where 5 - 25% of supplier's turnover, to minimise power/dependency issues); price; quality; speed of response; CSR and sustainability; e-commerce capability.
Supplier evaluation	Review current suppliers against the established qualifiers.
Supplier selection	• Consider retention of suppliers meeting *all* retention criteria and with capability to meet most performance qualifiers. • Check existing contractual obligations and notice periods • Consider using local suppliers on new product development and outsourced/global providers (when proven) • Use specifications that can be fulfilled by a number of suppliers, to maintain competition.
Implement-ation plan	• Develop a realistic time-phased plan for implementation. • Notify/feedback to de-selected suppliers professionally and ethically: leave door open to renewal (if appropriate) on defined improvement or capability development. • Amend vendor database, systems and codes accordingly.

Developing specifications

Specifications are a tool of communication with suppliers: conveying the buyer's needs to the supplier, and focusing communication for control and evaluation of what is delivered.

Specification of products/materials
Performance (basic operating characteristics)
Perceived quality (esteem value, brand position, reputation/image for quality)
Features (optional extras)
Conformance (key criteria/standards on which item must meet buyer's needs)
Reliability (rate of repair/maintenance)
Serviceability (ease of maintenance)
Aesthetics (pleasing appearance)
Durability (length of useful life)

Specification of services *(Parasuraman)*
Reliability (how consistently and dependably supplier provides the service)
Competence (skill and knowledge with which supplier staff supply service)
Courtesy (of supplier staff)
Understanding (supplier attempt to understand customer requirements)
Tangibles (physical goods as part of service)
Security (management of customer risk)
Credibility (supplier trustworthiness)
Access (how easy it is to contact supplier)
Responsiveness (prompt/willing service)

Lead role in specification

- **Purchasing:** eg if brand/samples available; items for internal use (eg factory clothing); purchasing staff expert.
- **User/engineering**: eg if technical expertise required.

Cross-functional interests

- Design: functionality
- Marketing: consumer acceptance, perceived value/benefits
- Manufacturing: economical production
- Procurement: materials availability, supplier capabilities, cost

NB: danger of marketing/user over-specification, unnecessary variety, expensive branded items > buyer role in questioning real needs, performance levels, tolerances.

Organisation approaches *(Dobler & Burt)*

- **Formal committee**: members represent interest groups > balance needs of different functions/user groups.
- **Informal**: buyers encouraged to challenge user assumptions, suggest alternatives; designers encouraged to seek buyer advice
- **Purchasing co-ordinator**: as informal, but purchasing staff designated as 'liaison officers' to facilitate required interactions.

Cross-functional involvement may extend to suppliers (next page).

Cross-functional involvement:

☑ Stakeholder interests and expertise represented
☑ Helps secure buy-in and purchasing/business integration
☑ Encourages integrated thinking/communication > improvement
☒ More costly and time-consuming than unilateral specification

Early supplier involvement (ESI)

Early supplier involvement is a process whereby suppliers are involved at an early stage in the product/service development process, enabling them to make proactive suggestions to improve designs and materials specifications.

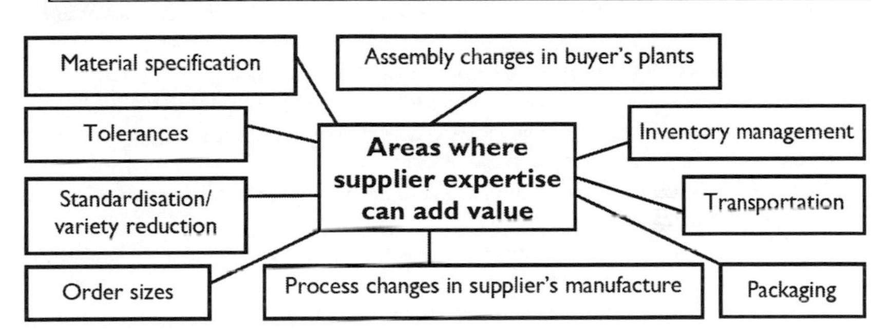

- ☑ Potential gains in cost, quality, development time/costs
- ☑ Reduced need for design/engineering changes at later stages
- ☑ Mutual clear understanding of capabilities/requirements > future development
- ☑ Potential to exploit supplier expertise/knowledge and up-to-date technology > product/service differentiation for competitive advantage
- ☑ Enhances supplier commitment as 'part of the team'
- ☑ Catalyst for developing long-term relationships > supply chain synergy, leverage
- ☑ Supports lean production (early, supply-chain wide elimination of wastes)

- ☒ Product/service may be designed/specified around the supplier (at expense of user requirements, flexibility, competition)
- ☒ Risk/cost if initial assessment of supplier capability (justification for ESI) exaggerated
- ☒ Not all suppliers suited (or adaptable) to demands of collaborative approach (may require supplier adoption support programmes/mentoring)
- ☒ Risk of exposing intellectual property and confidential data
- ☒ Potential conflicting objectives/interests of buyers/users/suppliers
- ☒ Risk of ESI suppliers becoming competitors

Simultaneous engineering: collaborative design and development using cross-functional internal teams and external suppliers.

Quality function deployment (QFD): design specification based on external and internal customer requirements. Scored on 'Whats' (features that customers require) + 'Hows' (characteristics of design enabling customer use) + Competitive performance (v two competing products).

In the Japanese model, QFD taskforces operate by genuine consensus decision-making: in Western settings, may require cultural change!

Communicating effectively with suppliers

- ❑ Key (high-influence, high-interest) stakeholders: need for early consultation, involvement, agreement > secure buy-in, commitment, co-operation
- ❑ Low-power, high-interest stakeholders (eg minor suppliers): keep informed
- ❑ Open information (eg on cost/price structures, precise requirements, policies and procedures) essential for collaboration, co-ordination, decision-making
- ❑ Honest disclosure (eg of anticipated problems, delays, disruptions or conflicts of interest) essential for risk management, problem solving, ethical/responsible dealings
- ❑ Free exchange of information supports creativity, innovation, collaborative problem-solving/improvement – and development of trust
- ❑ Constructive feedback on performance/relationship supports development, improvement, learning
- ❑ Open communication of need/plans for change helps secure buy-in, generate options, given socially responsible warning of impacts etc.
- ❑ Improve communication skills and systems in and between the organisations.

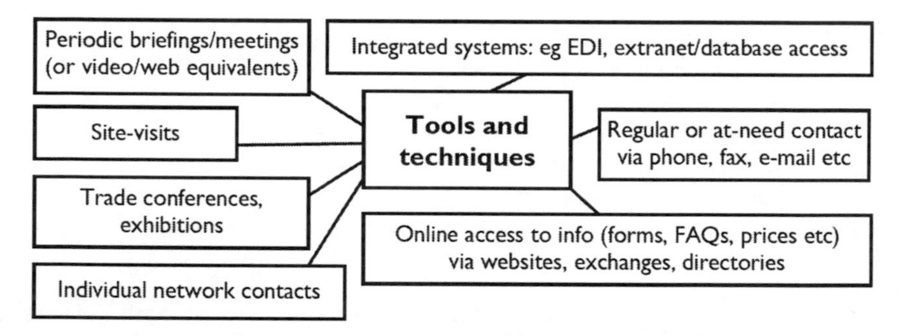

Supplier forums and associations

Supplier forums: regular meetings between buyers and (some or all) suppliers for discussion of issues of interest/concern. Framework for:

- Regular and open multi-directional communication > network co-operation
- Airing issues in co-operative atmosphere > support relationship
- Keeping suppliers informed re objectives, procedures, benchmarks, requirements etc
- Gathering supply market intelligence
- Best practice sharing

Supplier associations: special form of collaboration involving all players in supply network (buyer organisation, customers and suppliers).

- Best practice sharing > 'virtuous circle' of continuous improvement, waste reduction, value addition etc.
- Increased flow of information supports early supplier involvement
- Increase supply chain agility (flexibility, responsiveness)

Purchase cost reduction programme

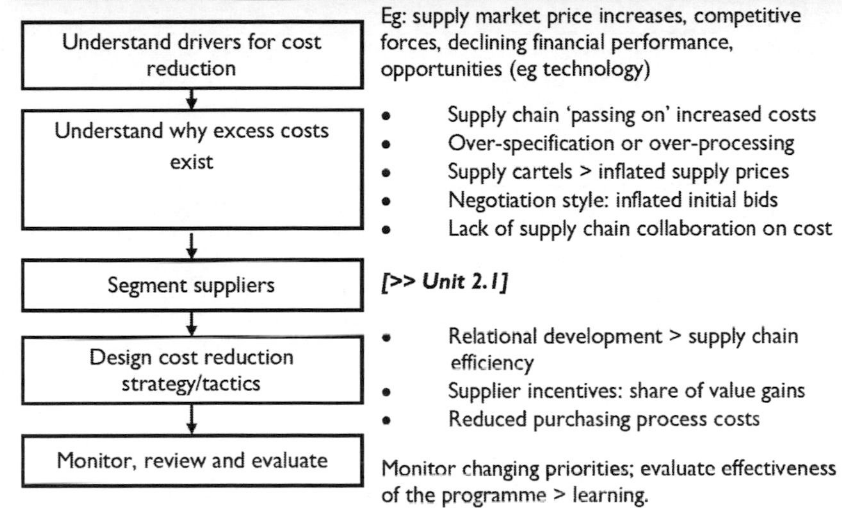

Checklist: some options for reducing purchasing costs

- ❑ Negotiate 'harder' on price (NB 'side effects' on quality, relationship etc)
- ❑ Reduce transaction/administration costs eg through: e-procurement, EDI, effective negotiation/tendering processes
- ❑ Use purchase cards: aggregrating small purchases, controlling 'maverick' spend
- ❑ Manage cashflow: extended credit terms from suppliers; prompt payment incentives to customers; use of consignment stock
- ❑ Negotiate volume and systems contracts: reduce small-value orders, 'maverick' spend
- ❑ Rationalise supply base > approved suppliers
- ❑ Source from low-cost countries (NB costs of quality/compliance management)
- ❑ Apply standardisation, variety reduction > consolidate requirements
- ❑ Consider consortium/collaborative purchasing (> volume discounts, price leverage)
- ❑ Buy generic spares rather than original equipment manufacturer (OEM) versions
- ❑ Consider outsourcing of non-core activities eg transport/logistics (NB costs/risks of management)
- ❑ Improved specification, demand management > purchase accurately to requirement
- ❑ Improved supplier and quality management > reduced inspection/defect costs
- ❑ Purchasing organisation: centralise (> savings from aggregated orders, bargaining leverage) or decentralise (> reduced transport/storage costs)

NB: designed to be useful for application in exam case studies – but ensure that any idea you recommend is relevant, suitable and practicable in the scenario given!

Volume and systems contracts

Spot buying	Buyer contacts supplier for one-off transactions as/when required. ☑ Simple/efficient (low transaction cost) where goods easily specified, goods needed immediately, order can be fulfilled immediately, agreed terms of trade exist. ☒ Risk of unfavourable spot price
Blanket ordering **Systems (block) contracts** **Cost/volume contracts**	**Blanket ordering:** supplier undertakes to provide estimated quantity of items over agreed period at agreed price or formula. As demand arises, buyers 'call off' requirements on agreed terms. **Systems contract** for larger group of items: master contract or catalogue fixes prices/terms. Supplier paid on periodic basis. **Cost and volume contracts** increasingly used in service environments. Added flexibility to purchase within agreed min/max parameters (improved responsiveness to demand). ☑ Increases purchasing leverage via aggregation of demand ☑ Reduced admin, streamlined delivery ☑ Reduced stock (supplier stores till needed: 'stockless purchasing') ☑ Can be user operated: frees purchasing staff > strategic roles ☑ Supplier benefits from guaranteed volume, improved capacity management, operational efficiencies ☒ Needs to be handled properly (eg realistic estimates of annual requirements, realistic order lead times) > obtain agreement ☒ Requires high degree of trust: contract on exclusive basis; supplier faces uncertain demand, stockholding, fast delivery etc

Stockless and just in time purchasing

Stockless purchasing is an arrangement under a systems contract whereby the supplier holds the inventory until the buyer calls off individual orders in response to immediate demand. The buying organisation holds no stock.

Just in time (JIT) purchasing is a more radical approach to inventory reduction, which 'provides for the cost-effective production and delivery of only the necessary quantity of parts at the right quantity, at the right time and place, while using the minimum amount of facilities, equipment, materials and human resources.' *(Voss)*

- ☑ Waste reduction, maximising added value, minimising cost
- ☑ Flexibility to meet variable demands and contingencies
- ☑ Reduced stock levels and lead times, higher quality, better customer service
- ☑ Employee involvement and empowerment > commitment, improvement
- ☑ Improved supply chain relationships, integrated systems
- ☒ Vulnerability to supplier/system failure: no time/stock buffers
- ☒ Reduction in capacity utilisation (trade-off with flexibility, customer satisfaction)

Features of JIT:

- ☐ **Adding value** eg by use of quality components, self-inspection of work in progress
- ☐ **Reducing waste** ('anything other than the minimum amount of equipment, materials, parts and working time essential to production', *Hay)*
- ☐ **Minimising inventory**: 'inventory is evil': incurs cost, hides operational inefficiencies
- ☐ **Supply chain flexibility**: late delivery, requiring integrated ICT systems, short supply lines and collaborative/partnership supply chain relationships
- ☐ **Simplification**: question the validity/purpose of any process that does not add value.
- ☐ **Quality**: commitment to quality at all tiers/stages: no rejects, reworks, inspection.
- ☐ **Speed:** make-to-order > speed of manufacture and throughput
- ☐ **Kaizen**: continuous incremental improvements
- ☐ **'Zero' target**: zero defects, lead-time, handling, set-up times, inventory

Customer-driven supply chain innovations

- ☐ **Supply chain** = creation of supply, or fulfilment > 'push' from supplier end
- ☐ **Demand chain** = creation of demand by market > 'pull' from customer end
  'Demand chain management would be a better term, and would stress the fact that the chain is driven by market forces and not by the supply side' *(Christopher).*

Marketing orientation: supply needs to be driven by demand. Supply relationships > value/quality chains.

- Communication systems (upstream, downstream, networked) for rapid response
- Value chain integration > optimise customer value along the supply chain
- Demand-focused product development/innovation (eg QFD approach)
- Cross-functional co-operation (and purchasing facilitation) for process alignment
- Supply chain agility (possibly at expense of lean production eg safety stocks to allow on demand delivery)

Balancing cost efficiency and other objectives

Measure 'total cost of ownership' (TOC) – not just 'price'. Trade offs eg:

- Price savings at expense of quality/risk (> added quality costs, reputational damage risk, relationship management costs)
- Discounts for bulk purchase (> added stockholding costs)
- Purchasing objectives (eg cost savings) v user/organisational objectives (eg quality, flexibility, speed) v supply chain objectives (eg long-term, gain-sharing relationships) v customer objectives (eg stock availability on demand, high quality specification).

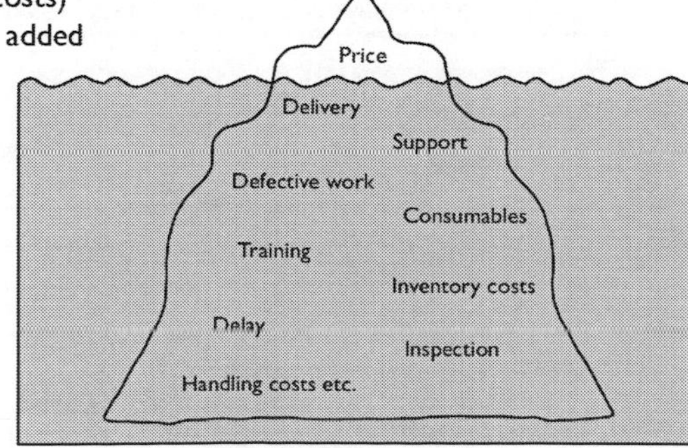

Tools of supplier performance appraisal (CIPS)

Systems and information tools	• Systems eg materials requirements planning (MRP), enterprise resource planning (ERP), performance monitoring software. • Info from suppliers, vendor database, buyer knowledge
Performance measurement and accreditation tools [>> Unit 1.2, 1.3]	• Vendor rating • Standard criteria eg Carter's 10Cs • Agreed key performance indicators • National/international standards and benchmarks
General management tools	• SWOT analysis: strengths/weaknesses of suppliers in relation to environmental opportunities/threats • Tools for prioritising supplies (eg ABC analysis) and type of supply relationships/KPIs best suited (eg *Kraljic matrix*)

Joint performance appraisal (JPA) approaches

Buyer and supplier assess each other's performance: focus on shared mutual objectives and measures, and problem-solving for mutual and relationship improvement. (NB costs and risk of transparency: only apply to priority suppliers.)

Key themes of JPA:

- Shared mutual objectives
- Agreed processes for problem-solving and identifying development needs
- Equitable sharing of risks and gains
- Continuous measurable improvements
- Proactively managed relationship

☑ Joint performance measures > focus on mutual benefits and value gains
☑ Motivates both parties to seek improvements (and integrates > process alignment)
☑ Mutual understanding of each other's aims, constraints > problem solving
☑ Ethical, relationship-building approach: minimises dominance/exploitation issues
☑ Supports supply chain perspective: weighs overall efficiency and competitive power of total supply chain (not just individual organisations)
☑ Operational/process gains eg cost efficiency, quality, delivery, secure supply etc.

Use of both quantitative and qualitative measures

Quantitative measures	Qualitative measures
Easier to define KPIs, monitor over time	KPIs, monitoring likely to be subjective
Focus on efficiency	Focus on effectiveness
Suit purchase of products (tangibles)	Suit purchase of services (intangibles)
Eg price, total cost of ownership, on-time-in-full deliveries, error/defect rates etc ***[>> Unit 1.3]***	Eg customer satisfaction; management/HR capability; willingness to collaborate, improve; cultural compatibility; R & D/innovation capability; ethical/CSR values; level of technological development

Stakeholder input to supplier performance appraisal

- ❑ **Cross-functional teams** from both organisations are often used in JPA to monitor, review and analyse results on a periodic basis.
- ❑ **360-degree feedback (multi-source appraisal):** assessment of performance by a range of relevant stakeholders > rounded, representative viewpoint on performance

- ☑ Represent different stakeholder interests and viewpoints
- ☑ Contribute different specialist expertise (eg financial to interpret financial ratios)
- ☑ Stakeholder involvement and buy-in to improvement/development plans
- ☑ Improved potential for integrated/synergistic solutions
- ☑ Supports open relational culture and communication

Stakeholder	***Interest in supplier performance***	***Contribution to appraisal***
Purchasing	Support for own performance; credibility/status in organisation; potential to develop effective supply chain strategies	Overall responsibility; leadership and management; coordination and implementation; review and feedback
Suppliers	Own competitive advantage, reputation, survival/growth, retained goodwill/custom of buyer, potential for sharing value gains	Provision of measurement data; ideas for improvement; feedback on buyer's performance; in some cases, self-assessment
User/other departments	Fulfilment of requirements; costs of meeting requirements; potential for added value, synergy, innovation	Input re criteria; technical expertise; feedback on supplier performance
External third parties	Ethical trading and employment; consumer rights; security and pricing of supply (eg for essential services), statutory reports/returns, environment protection etc.	Influence on KPIs used (eg public sector compulsory competitive tendering, CSR/ethical codes); input to design of appraisal (eg consultants).

Supplier business continuity planning (BCP)

Business continuity planning is designed to identify potential threats to critical activities, and ensure that business functions can be maintained. It includes issues such as management succession, systems changeover and disaster recovery (measures to restore service following major disruption eg fire, IT systems failure, departure of key personnel).

- ☑ Identification of critical systems and vulnerabilities to prioritise counter-measures
- ☑ Defined roles and responsibilities > swift, co-ordinated response in emergency
- ☑ Preparation of plans/resources to maintain minimum acceptable level of service
- ☑ Opportunities for buyer input (risk assessment, guarantees) to protect interests
- ☑ Time to develop resources and skills (eg lead time for management development)
- ☑ Imposes rigour on system/product/relationship design to build in resilience
- ☑ Improved risk awareness and management through supply chain

2.5 Analyse different supply markets and conditions, and liaise to co-ordinate inbound logistics and materials flows

Logistics management

Logistics is 'the process of strategically managing the cost-effective movement and storage of materials, parts and finished inventory from suppliers, through the firm and onto customers'. *(Christopher)*

Tasks of logistics management
Demand forecasting and planning
Order processing for info exchange
Customer service: co-ordination of product allocation/distribution
Purchasing & inventory management
Materials handling: minimising non-value adding movement
Warehousing: design of storage/picking
Transportation
Design of ICT/communication linkages

Key factors in logistics strategy
Customer service: market needs as key driver of logistics systems.
Cost minimisation (profitability) > order processing, optimum no./location/layout of stores, inventory deployment, outsourcing.
Info systems: eg transparency, whole-chain demand management, track and trace
Organisation structure: horizontal process integration, potential outsource
CSR: H & S, environment, compliance

- **Push logistics:** supply chain activities based on demand forecasts > allows economies of scale, safety stock for customer needs – but potential over-production.
- **Pull logistics**: supply chain activities based on actual demand, customer orders > reduced inventory – but requires short lead times, loses economies of scale.
- **Push-pull logistics**: front end push oriented to maximise customer service + decoupled upstream reacting to actual customer demand, to minimise inventory.
- **Reverse logistics** (closed loop supply chain): moving goods, packaging, equipment and info *back from point of sale* eg for waste disposal, re-use, recycling, product recalls/returns, repair/maintenance services.

Integration of purchasing accountabilities > materials management > logistics:

☑ Cost reduction through eliminating waste at all stages of the process
☑ More systematic planning, co-ordination and control
☑ Greater supply chain flexibility and responsiveness to customer demands
☑ Reconciling of conflicting sub-unit objectives
☑ Support for world class approaches eg JIT, TQM.

Benchmarking logistics performance

Benchmark (eg SCOR): compare key **metrics** (eg supply chain reliability, responsiveness, flexibility, cost, asset management) across five **supply chain activities**:

- **Plan**: balance aggregate demand/supply to meet sourcing/production/delivery needs
- **Source**: procure goods and services to meet planned or actual demand
- **Make**: transform product to finished state to meet planned or actual demand
- **Deliver**: provide finished products (order, transportation, distribution management)
- **Return:** process associated with returning or receiving returned products.

Benchmarking priorities *(Walleck)*:

- ❑ Supply chain processes/entities that are of strategic importance
- ❑ Supply chain processes/entities that have a high relative impact on the business
- ❑ Areas where there is a choice between make and buy
- ❑ Areas where there is internal readiness to implement change

Supply chain process flow documentation

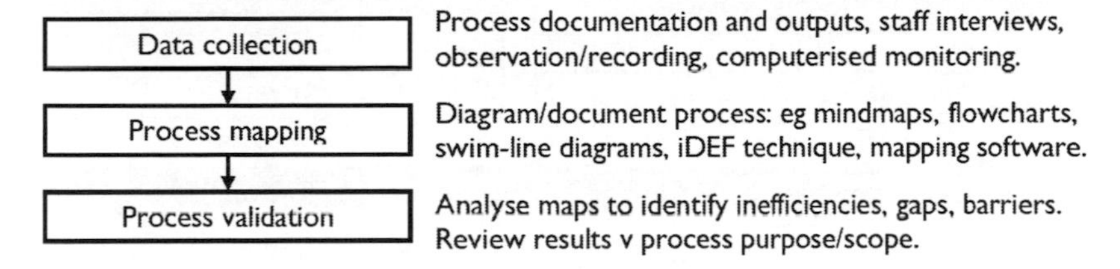

Data collection: Process documentation and outputs, staff interviews, observation/recording, computerised monitoring.

Process mapping: Diagram/document process: eg mindmaps, flowcharts, swim-line diagrams, iDEF technique, mapping software.

Process validation: Analyse maps to identify inefficiencies, gaps, barriers. Review results v process purpose/scope.

- ❑ **Swim lane diagrams**: flow diagram within horizontal channels depicting units responsible. Focuses on interfaces + high-risk points of transfer between units.
- ❑ **ICAM DEFinition language (iDEF)**: Process function boxes linked > map entire process. Easy to use (limited set of notations) + more complex variants to support different requirements (eg time dependency). Requires detailed analysis.

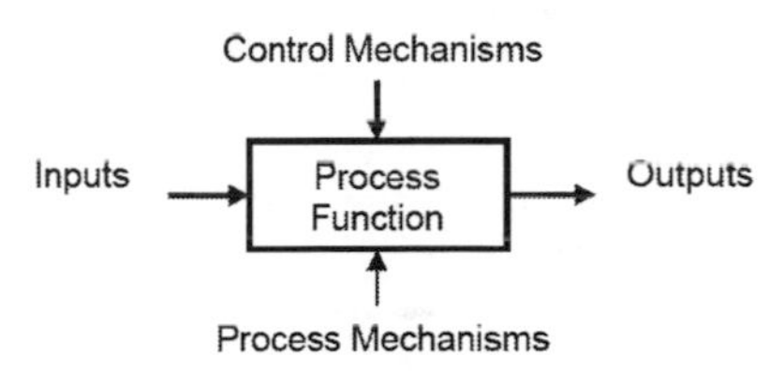

Process analysis and documentation:

- ☑ Involves process owners > improves understanding, gains buy-in for change
- ☑ Facilitates identification of bottlenecks, gaps, non-value adding activities
- ☑ Supports staff participation in learning, improvement, innovation
- ☑ Clarifies interdependencies between functions/supply chain entities > collaboration
- ☑ Emphasises process flow/alignment > customer value

Business process re-engineering (BPR)

Business process re-engineering (BPR) is 'the fundamental rethinking and radical redesign of business processes to achieve dramatic improvement in critical, contemporary measures of performance, such as cost, quality, service and speed.' *(Hammer & Champy)*

- ☑ Revolutionary thinking (paradigm shift > transformational change)
- ☑ Breakthrough improvements (radical quality/cost gains)
- ☑ Aligned horizontal structures > facilitate customer satisfaction
- ☑ Lean structures: cut low-value activities, automate, outsource
- ☑ Culture > facilitate/empower, customer focus, organisational learning
- ☑ Job redesign > output focused, integrated, meaningful (whole-process) tasks
- ☑ ICT leverage > integration, automation of activities not requiring human input

2.5 Analyse different supply markets and conditions, and liaise to co-ordinate inbound logistics and materials flows

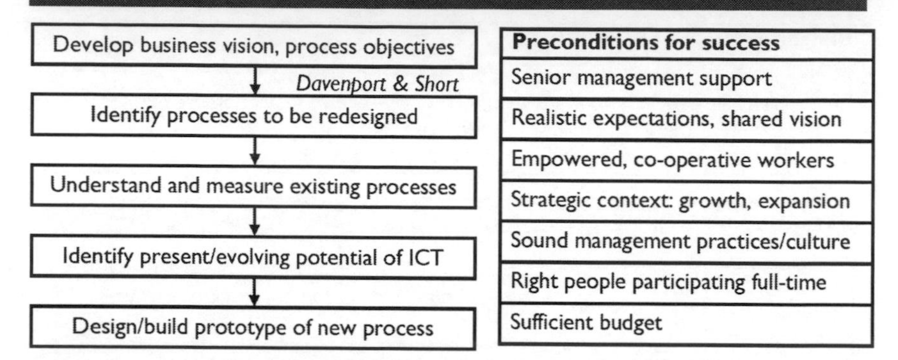

Preconditions for success
Senior management support
Realistic expectations, shared vision
Empowered, co-operative workers
Strategic context: growth, expansion
Sound management practices/culture
Right people participating full-time
Sufficient budget

Lean supply

Lean thinking focuses on reducing costs and maximising added value through: quality improvement; elimination of waste (activities which add cost but not value); employee involvement; and collaborative supply chain relationships.

	Seven wastes *(Ohno)*
1	**Over-production**
2	**Excess inventory**
3	**Transportation**
4	**Waiting**
5	**Unnecessary motion**
6	**Over-processing**
7	**Correction**

Key values of lean thinking
Specify value creation from customer viewpoint
Identify all steps across value stream (process map)
Ensure flow of actions that create value
Remove non-value-added steps from operations
Only make what is customer pulled, just in time
Practise continuous improvement + waste removal
Use cross-functional teams and involve employees

Benefits of lean
Progressive removal of wastes
Collaborative relationships > synergy
Cross-functional teams > flexibility
Reduced inventories > better cash flow
Shorter cycle/delivery times
More efficient resource utilisation
Fewer defects > lower failure costs

Limitations of lean
Reduced capability to respond flexibly to contingencies
Lean supply chains > increased supply risk and reduced opportunism
Short-term cost-reduction focus
Vulnerability of less powerful partners
Suits high-volume, predictable demand

Agile thinking involves developing the ability to respond swiftly to change and contingencies (eg supplier failure, urgent orders). The focus of agile strategy is developing supply chain flexibility for service and customer value enhancement.

- Streamlining the physical in-flow of parts/materials from suppliers
- Streamlining/integrating the flow of information (eg through EDI)
- Fast response > product modification, shorter product lifecycles
- Acceptance of inventory (unlike lean supply) where necessary to add value (eg through fast delivery response, work-in-progress held for late customisation)

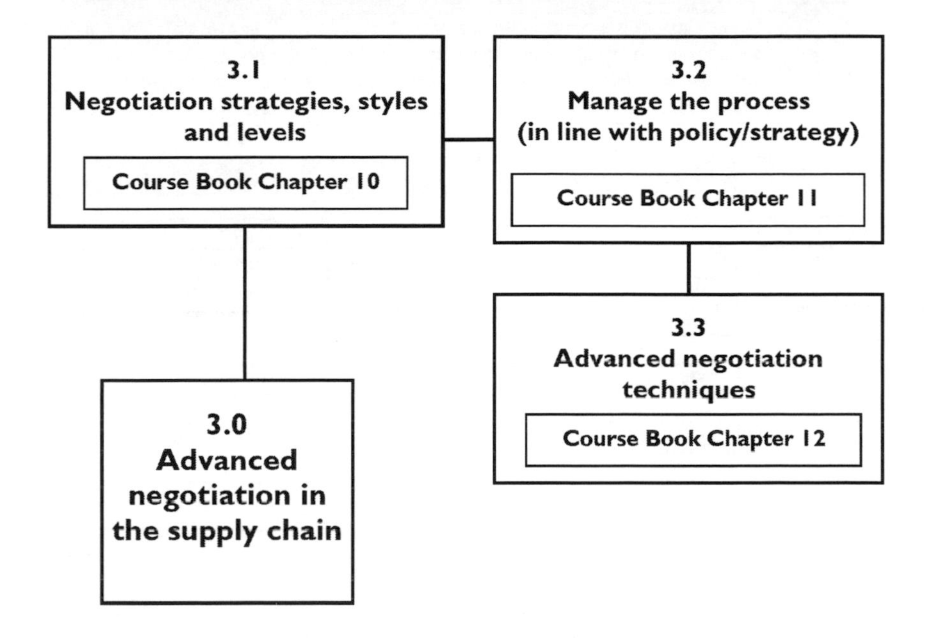
3.1
Negotiation strategies, styles and levels
Course Book Chapter 10
3.2
Manage the process (in line with policy/strategy)
Course Book Chapter 11
3.3
Advanced negotiation techniques
Course Book Chapter 12
3.0
Advanced negotiation in the supply chain

3.1 Evaluate different negotiation strategies, styles and levels; formulate appropriate strategies

Negotiation is a process where two parties come together to confer, in a situation in which there is some conflict of interests between them, with a view to concluding a jointly acceptable agreement. It can be applied in a range of contexts, including commercial negotiations and general conflict resolution.

Phases of negotiation

(Kennedy)
Prepare
Argue
Signal
Propose
Package
Bargain
Close
Agree

Prepare: what do *we* want?

Debate: what do *they* want?

Propose: what wants *might* we trade?

Bargain: what wants *will* we trade?

(Greenhalgh)
Preparation
Relationship building
Info gathering
Info using
Bidding
Closing the deal
Implementing agreement

- ❑ **Prepare** — Pre-negotiation planning: establish **objectives** and **priorities** (Must, Intend, Like); gather info to build a negotiating position and anticipate opposing positions; determine the **range of negotiation** and agree range of responses to variables (negotiable/non-negotiable items, bargaining 'currencies' or tradeable items, minimum acceptable positions); plan timing, resourcing and management of negotiation meeting; plan tactics, ploys and roles within the **negotiating team**.
- ❑ **Open**. — Each side **presents** its position, case or opening bid (where possible, inducing a 'marker' from the other party first, prior to stating one's own desired outcome)
- ❑ **Test**. — Each side feels out the other's **position**, gauging potential for mutual gains or trading of concessions, determining areas of strength/weaknesses etc.
- ❑ **Move**. — Each side uses available tactics to coerce or influence movement in the other party's position towards a mutually acceptable position: **unilateral** movement (eg by applying coercion or incentives) or **mutual** movement (eg by trading concessions)
- ❑ **Agree**. — Various tactics are used to 'close' the deal > both sides accept the closing position (or walk away, if there is an acceptable alternative or BATNA) > **written summary** agreed by the meeting.
- ❑ **Finalise the deal**. — The agreement is **ratified** (eg by a Board of Directors) and embodied in a formal **document** for signature by both sides. This is the basis of implementation and performance monitoring (or contract management).

Behavioural attributes of skilled negotiators *(Rackham)*

During pre-negotiation planning:
Considered a wider range of outcome options Spent more time looking for areas of potential common ground Thought more about the long-term implications of issues Prepared their goals around ranges rather than fixed positions Focused on individual issues, rather than the sequence in which they might be covered
During face-to-face interaction:
Made fewer immediate counter-proposals Were less likely to describe their offers in exaggeratedly positive terms Avoided defend-attack cycles Used behavioural labelling (except when disagreeing) and feelings commentary Tested understanding and summarised points/progress Used fewer, stronger arguments to back up their arguments (rather than diluting them)
During post-negotiation review
Set aside time to review what they learned from the negotiation

- Need for **teamwork** in negotiation teams
- Need for **trust** and **rapport**: attention to human factors

Negotiation styles in different supply chain contexts

Competitive relationship	**Collaborative relationship**
Buying organisation seeks to obtain the best price possible, at the expense of the supplier's profit margin (and *vice versa*).	Buying organisation seeks to develop long-term relationship with supplier: work together to add value, to mutual benefit.
Distributive (win-lose) negotiation	**Integrative** (win-win) negotiation

> **Prioritise** relationships/suppliers (using Kraljic, Pareto) > select appropriate approach.

Distributive negotiation approach	**Integrative negotiation approach**
Bargaining > distribution of limited resources: 'dividing up a fixed pie' > zero-sum, win-lose or competitive outcome.	Collaborative problem-solving to increase options available ('expand the pie'): seek mutually satisfying or added-value solutions ('win-win').
• Exaggerated initial positions/demands • Polarise conflicting positions • Withholding info on common ground • 'Closed book' (no cost info sharing) • Using levers to coerce, manipulate other party to make concessions • Offering minimal return concessions • Never making the first concession • Over-state own concessions	• Openness about needs/concerns • 'Open book' (cost info sharing) • Generating options with genuine mutual or trade-off benefits • Focusing on areas of common ground • Supporting other party in accepting • Modelling flexibility re counter-offers • Using concessions to build trust (unilateral, if clearly acknowledged, relatively low-risk, justifiable: *Malhotra*)

3.1 Evaluate different negotiation strategies, styles and levels; formulate appropriate strategies

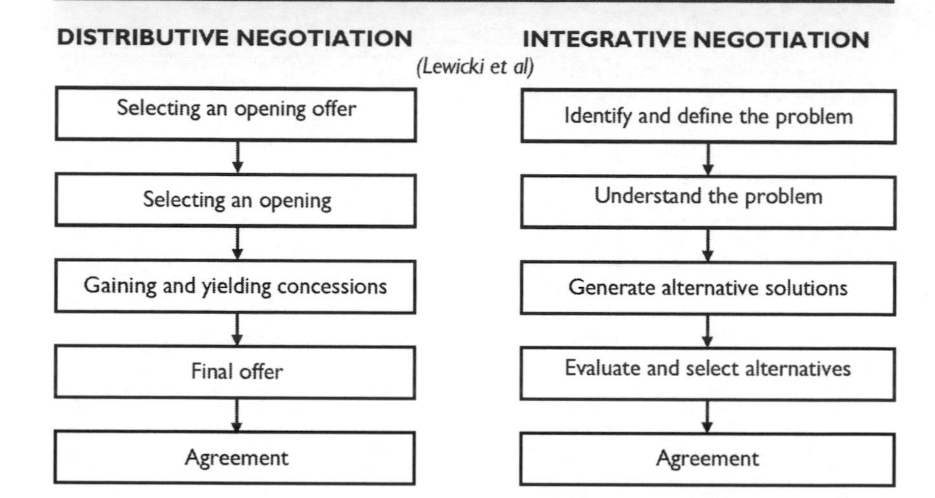

Open book negotiation

Open book negotiation is based on visibility of the supplier's costs, in order to allow both parties to agree acceptable profit margins and work together on mutually advantageous cost reductions.

Open book costing (and negotiation)	Supplier provides buyer with information about costs. ☑ Reassures re value for money (not exploitative profit margins) ☑ Facilitates cost-based pricing ☑ Enables buyer to get to know supplier operations/processes ☑ Enables identification of areas for cost reduction, value adding ☒ Flow of costing info one-way: reflects buyer dominance ☒ Risk to commercially sensitive information ☒ Suppliers may protect interests by providing inaccurate data ☒ Supplier may not share value added (in adversarial relationship)
Cost transparency	Customer and supplier share two-way cost information, for activities in which they have a common interest. ☑ Enables identification of areas for cost reduction ☑ Enables mutual understanding of objectives, constraints ☑ Encourages closer collaboration for mutual benefit ☑ Suits strategic relationships (with confidentiality protection)

A **dispute** is an area of disagreement between a buyer and supplier: it may not imply any form of relational **conflict** (hostility).

Continuum of dispute resolution techniques:

Decision by negotiators				*3rd party decision*		*Legal decision*	
Avoidance	Discussion /problem solving	Informal negoti-ation	Conciliation or Mediation	Admin. decision	Arbitration	Judicial decision	Legisl-ative decision

Escalation (higher level, more adversarial intensity) →

Disputes should be addressed at the lowest/soonest possible level, prior to escalation (referral upwards) to higher levels. **Escalation routes** (*OGC*):

Informal discussion > negotiated settlement (escalation from buyer-supplier > functional managers > executive sponsors) > mediation > neutral evaluation > expert determination > arbitration/adjudication > litigation.

Alternative dispute resolution (ADR)

Conciliation: disputes are aired in discussion facilitated by an impartial conciliator, whose role is to manage the process and identify potential areas of movement toward settlement – *not* to make judgements. A typical conciliation process includes:

- Fact-finding, (often in individual meetings with conciliator)
- Joint meetings, to explain positions and identify areas of conflict and common ground
- Negotiation towards a mutually acceptable position, if possible.

Mediation may follow conciliation, if a voluntary settlement has not been reached. It involves the appointment of an independent person (or panel) who will:

- Consider the case of both sides (set out in writing)
- Hear evidence and arguments at a mediation hearing
- Make a formal proposal or recommendation (not binding) as a basis for settlement

☑ Less costly/time-consuming (relatively little 'mechanism') than litigation/arbitration
☑ Confidential/private (including independent meetings, where required)
☑ Non-adversarial: designed to promote ongoing business relationships
☑ Input from neutral third party specifically skilled in constructive *process*

☒ Does not necessarily result in 'best' outcome for a given party
☒ Third party is not necessarily expert in contract subject matter
☒ Decisions are not binding: issues may go unresolved (or go to arbitration/litigation)

Arbitration and adjudication

Arbitration is a more formal approach to resolving disputes, governed by statute (Arbitration Act 1996). Both sides agree to be bound by the decision of a nominated third party (arbitrator), often following court-style proceedings. (Most commonly used procedure for international disputes, with arbitration services, agreed rules/enforcement, and neutrality re place, language used, procedures/law applied etc.)

Contractual **arbitration agreements** include agreement to refer disputes to arbitration and time limits during which arbitration must begin.

The term '**adjudication**' is used almost exclusively for dispute resolution under Part II of the *Housing Grants, Construction and Regeneration Act* (HGCRA) 1996.

Role of purchasing in resolving disputes

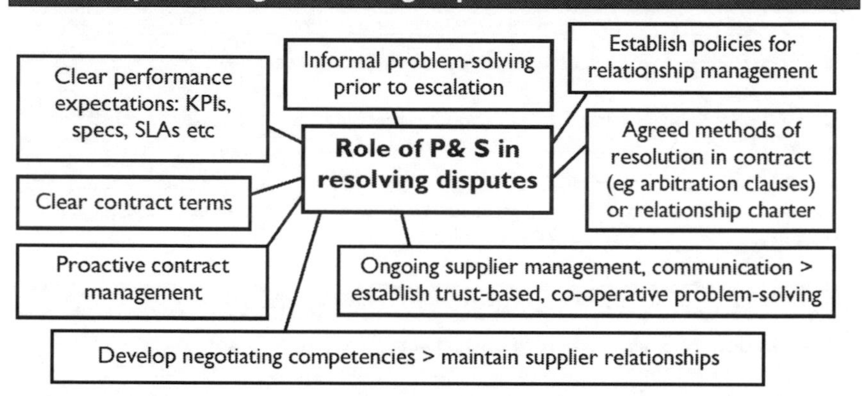

Managing conflict in negotiations

Managing potential conflicts: the breakthrough approach (*Ury*)

Barriers to co-operation	Challenge	Strategy
Your reaction to others	Don't react	Mentally distance yourself
Other's negative emotions	Disarm them	Respond with empathy
Others' positional behaviour	Change the game	Don't reject: reframe the issue > open more options
Others' scepticism about benefits of agreement	Make it easy to say 'yes'	Make an offer that is easy to assent to
Other's perceived power	Make it hard to say 'no'	Show you have a BATNA

Thomas model of conflict handling styles:

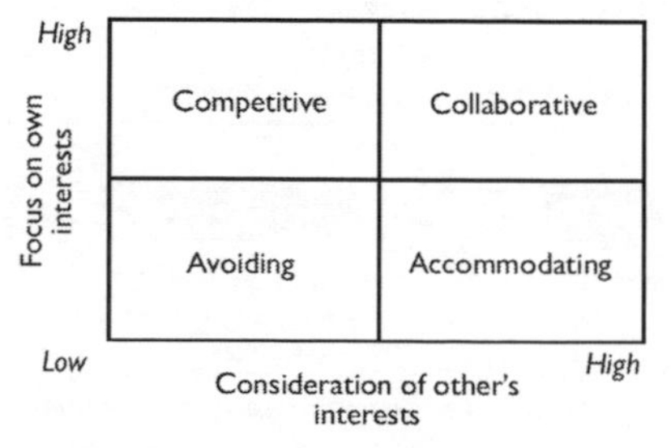

- **Avoiding**: you withdraw from conflict: attempt to sweep under the carpet
- **Competing**: you impose your solution on the problem.
- **Accommodating**: you concede the issue, to preserve harmony
- **Collaborating:** both parties work to find 'win-win' to clearly stated needs.

Designing and developing a negotiation plan

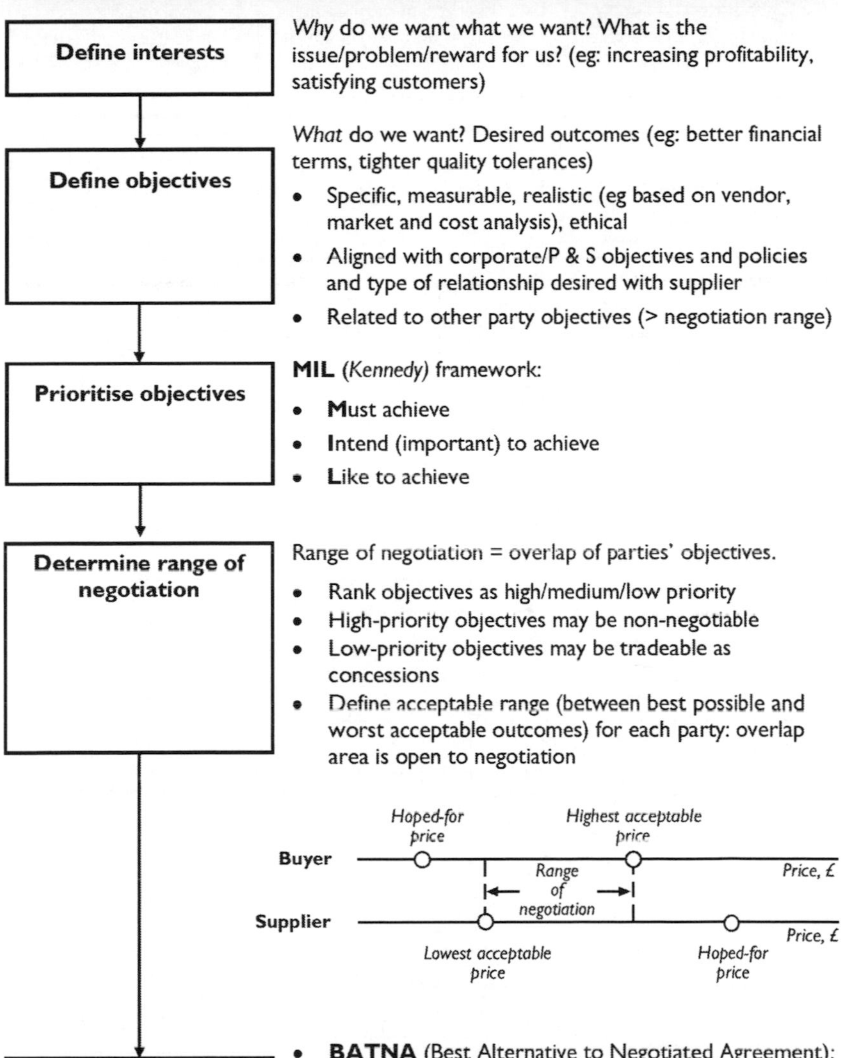

Define interests

Why do we want what we want? What is the issue/problem/reward for us? (eg: increasing profitability, satisfying customers)

Define objectives

What do we want? Desired outcomes (eg: better financial terms, tighter quality tolerances)

- Specific, measurable, realistic (eg based on vendor, market and cost analysis), ethical
- Aligned with corporate/P & S objectives and policies and type of relationship desired with supplier
- Related to other party objectives (> negotiation range)

Prioritise objectives

MIL (*Kennedy*) framework:

- **M**ust achieve
- **I**ntend (important) to achieve
- **L**ike to achieve

Determine range of negotiation

Range of negotiation = overlap of parties' objectives.

- Rank objectives as high/medium/low priority
- High-priority objectives may be non-negotiable
- Low-priority objectives may be tradeable as concessions
- Define acceptable range (between best possible and worst acceptable outcomes) for each party: overlap area is open to negotiation

Determine alternatives to negotiated agreement

- **BATNA** (Best Alternative to Negotiated Agreement): acceptable Plan B, if agreement cannot be reached (back-up alternative > supports walk away)
- **Walk-away position** (or 'resistance point'): point beyond which terms are unacceptable: if no further movement > walk away

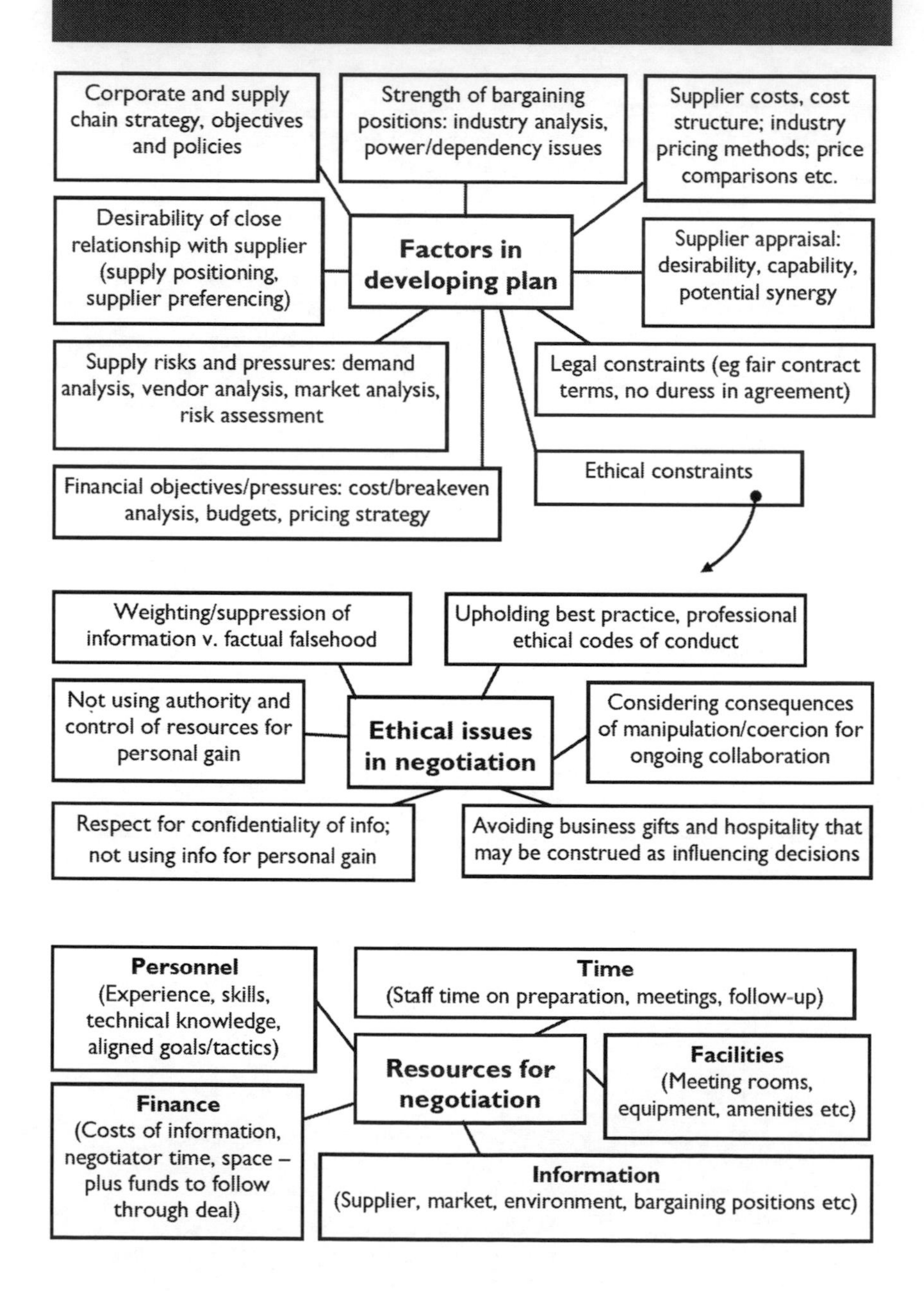
Corporate and supply chain strategy, objectives and policies
Strength of bargaining positions: industry analysis, power/dependency issues
Supplier costs, cost structure; industry pricing methods; price comparisons etc.
Desirability of close relationship with supplier (supply positioning, supplier preferencing)
Factors in developing plan
Supplier appraisal: desirability, capability, potential synergy
Supply risks and pressures: demand analysis, vendor analysis, market analysis, risk assessment
Legal constraints (eg fair contract terms, no duress in agreement)
Financial objectives/pressures: cost/breakeven analysis, budgets, pricing strategy
Ethical constraints
Weighting/suppression of information v. factual falsehood
Upholding best practice, professional ethical codes of conduct
Not using authority and control of resources for personal gain
Ethical issues in negotiation
Considering consequences of manipulation/coercion for ongoing collaboration
Respect for confidentiality of info; not using info for personal gain
Avoiding business gifts and hospitality that may be construed as influencing decisions
Personnel
(Experience, skills, technical knowledge, aligned goals/tactics)
Time
(Staff time on preparation, meetings, follow-up)
Resources for negotiation
Facilities
(Meeting rooms, equipment, amenities etc)
Finance
(Costs of information, negotiator time, space – plus funds to follow through deal)
Information
(Supplier, market, environment, bargaining positions etc)

Building and maintaining rapport

Rapport is the sense of relationship or connection we have when we relate to other people.

- ☑ Helps establish openness and trust
- ☑ Supports influencing through pacing and leading (establishing empathy/trust before reframing/changing); creating trust/liking; overcoming barriers

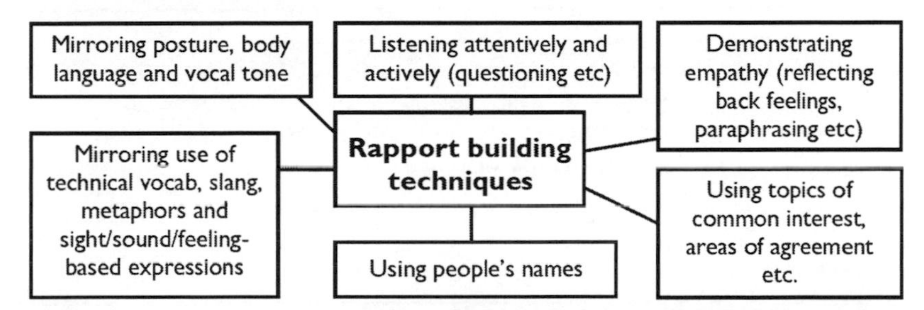

Influencing techniques

Influencing is the process of applying some form of pressure in order to change other people's attitudes or behaviours: to secure their compliance, obedience, conformity or commitment.

Persuasion is influencing *other* than by the use of power: it aims to pull or lead people to change by aligning their beliefs and goals with those of the influencer.

Effective persuasive communication > 'central route to influence' *(Lewicki et al):*

Content	Structure	Style
Attractive offer	Break down complex issues	Encourage participation
Expressed to make it easy to say 'yes'	Present argument from both sides	Use metaphors to draw attention
Congruent with other party's values	Repeat the message	Provoke emotional responses
Suggest 'agreement in principle'	Conclude the argument	Say the unexpected

Verbal tools
Polarised language (we are 'co-operative'; they are 'unreasonable')
Immediate, compelling language
Power relationship expression (assertive clarity/firmness: high power)
Label positive behaviours ('I'd like to make a suggestion…'> control processes)
Test understanding ('Do I understand that you're saying…?') and summarising
Ask specific, probing questions (in appropriate styles)
Know 'when to answer, when not to answer, when to answer clearly and when to answer vaguely' *(Dobler et al)*

3.3 Explain advanced negotiation techniques

Active listening
Attentive body language, eye contact
Giving encouraging feedback
Questions, summaries etc for dialogue
Keeping an open mind
Being patient > maintain focus
Paying attention to non-verbal cues

Non-verbal cues
Kinesic behaviour (body language): gesture, facial expression, appropriate eye contact
Proxemics (nearness) and posture
Paralanguage: tone of voice, pauses, silences etc
Object language (grooming, symbols etc)

Transactional analysis *(Berne)*

Analysis of single stimulus-response communication exchanges (transactions) to understand 'where people are coming from' and how/why they respond as they do.

People act/respond out of one of three **ego states**:

- **Parent** (P): based on parents' behaviour (critical or nurturing): *taught* concept of life
- **Child** (C): memory of own childhood feelings/thoughts: *felt* concept of life
- **Adult** (A): rational response to present/actual events: *thought* concept of life

- ❑ **Assess which state** parties are acting from: 'crossed transactions' may explain conflicts; Adult/Child states may explain irrational positions, unwillingness to move
- ❑ **Use states** to guide negotiation process: eg move to Parent to elicit Child response (coercive influencing), or shift both parties to Adult (rational persuasion, conflict management), or shift both parties to Child (creative brainstorming).
- ❑ Increase **self-awareness** of own behaviours, in order to develop more intentional responses > achieve results you want.

Game theory

- ❑ 'Game': players; possible moves (strategies); payoffs (+ve, -ve) from moves adopted.
- ❑ 'One-shot games' (move-countermove) or multiple moves: strategy adjustments, feedback etc.
- ❑ Behaviour based on incentives to change strategy in response to range of outcomes
- ❑ Non-zero-sum game (eg Prisoner's Dilemma): *collaboration* may maximise payoff for both players (eg increase the size of the pie)
- ❑ Outcomes may be improved by dealing with same player over time: maximise feedback, learning, improvement.

Negotiating in established collaborative relationships

- ❑ **Integrative** (win-win) bargaining – not distributive (zero-sum) ***[>>Unit 3.1]***
- ❑ **Ethical** ('pull') influencing – not manipulative ('push') style ***[>> Unit 3.2]***
- ❑ **Principled negotiation** *(Fisher & Ury):* hard (on the problem: deciding issues on objective merits, standing up for legitimate rights and interests) and soft (on the people: looking for mutual gains, fairness of debate and outcome). Separate people from problem; focus on reconciling interests (needs, concerns, fears) rather than positions; generating variety of ideas/options (expand the pie before dividing it); insist that agreement reflect objectively fair standard (eg market value, reciprocity, KPIs)

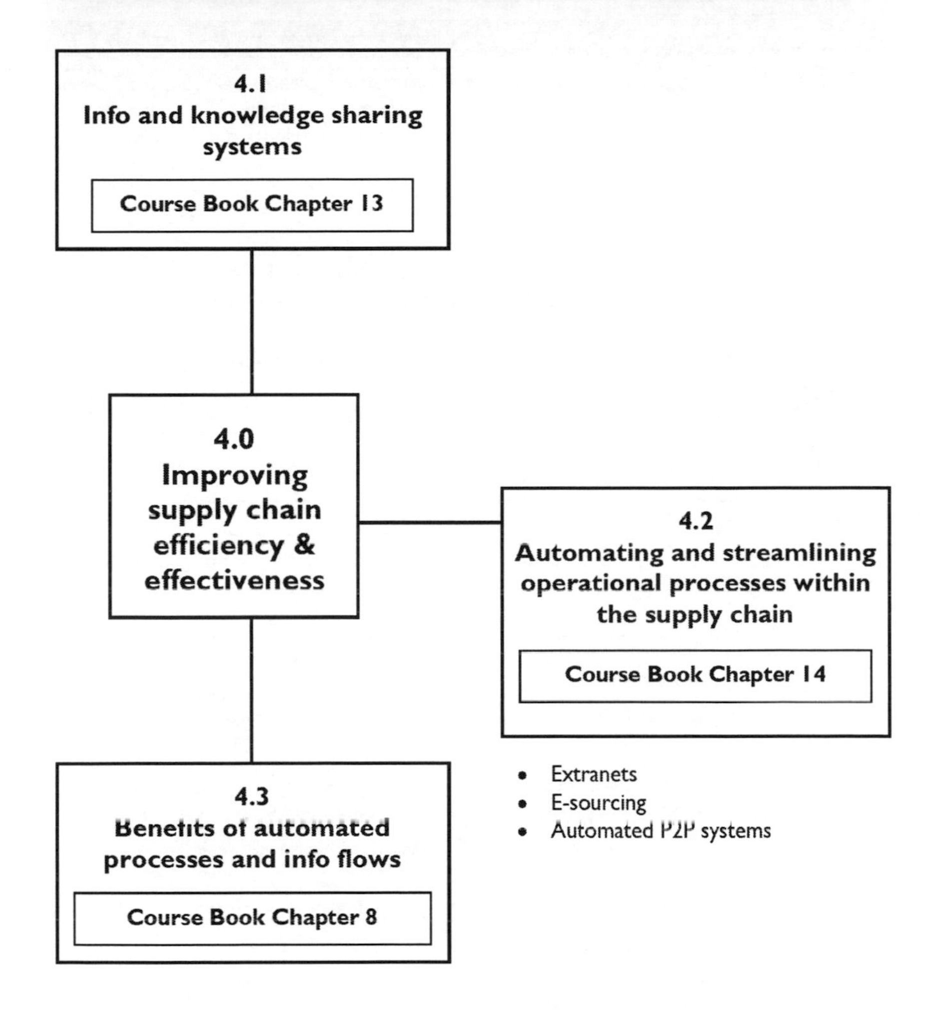
4.1
Info and knowledge sharing systems
Course Book Chapter 13
4.0
Improving supply chain efficiency & effectiveness
4.2
Automating and streamlining operational processes within the supply chain
Course Book Chapter 14
4.3
Benefits of automated processes and info flows
Course Book Chapter 8
Extranets
E-sourcing
Automated P2P systems

4.1 Develop and implement appropriate information and knowledge sharing systems between purchasing departments and suppliers

Knowledge management

Knowledge management is the organisation, creation, sharing and flow of knowledge within organisations. Its objective is to optimise the knowledge that is available in an organisation, create new knowledge and increase awareness and understanding.

>> Identification, capture and transfer of learning:

- From one purchasing project/initiative to another
- Within internal supply chains (ie cross-functional knowledge sharing)
- Between buyers and members of the external supply network
- From external info sources (eg benchmark standards)
- Within knowledge communities (eg professional/industry bodies).

A **knowledge community** is a group of individuals or organisations with a common interest and a willingness to share ideas and experience for mutual learning – eg via personal contact or ICT links ('virtual' global community).

The Nonaka-Takeuchi model

- Organisational learning results from individual knowledge being transferred, enlarged and shared upwards to the organisational level.

	Tacit	Tacit	
Tacit	SOCIALISATION From tacit to tacit Sharing experiences, mental models and skills	EXTERNALISATION From tacit to explicit Articulating tacit knowledge into concepts	Explicit
Tacit	INTERNALISATION From explicit to tacit Embodying explicit knowledge into tacit knowledge	COMBINATION From explicit to explicit Systemising concepts into known systems	Explicit
	Explicit	Explicit	

- **Socialisation**: tacit knowledge transferred through interactions between people
- **Externalisation:** tacit knowledge articulated (by metaphor/analogy) > explicit (for formalising and sharing with others)
- **Combination:** multiple examples of explicit knowledge aggregated (by meetings, discussion groups, documented histories etc)
- **Internalisation:** explicit knowledge > tacit (by reflection, repetition, absorption)

Management information systems (MIS)

Management information systems (MIS) are systems that take information captured by transaction processing systems (eg EPOS) and produce reports to support managerial planning and control.

Hardware	Software	People/users	Communication links	Data

Develop and implement appropriate information and knowledge sharing systems between purchasing departments and suppliers **4.1**

- ❑ Inventory, work-in-progress, repair/maintenance and supply chain data (operations records) > production schedules, inventory systems, production monitoring systems
- ❑ Staff, appraisal, salary data (HR records) > employee performance and HR reports
- ❑ Business intelligence, competitor, environmental data (strategic records) > industry trend reports, portfolio models, purchasing research reports etc

Decision support systems	Allow users to consider contingency planning ('what if?') scenarios > select best options
Strategic support systems	Allow users to measure/evaluate performance, analyse benchmarking data, receive exception reports
Enterprise resource planning	'Computer-based systems designed to process an organisation's transactions and facilitate integrated and real time planning, production and customer response' *(CIPS)*. Cross-functional, enterprise-wide integration.
Supplier/vendor database	Centralised collection of structured data, organised so that different users can access/interrogate it according to information needs > supplier selection, performance/contract/relationship management.

Buyer-supplier communication links

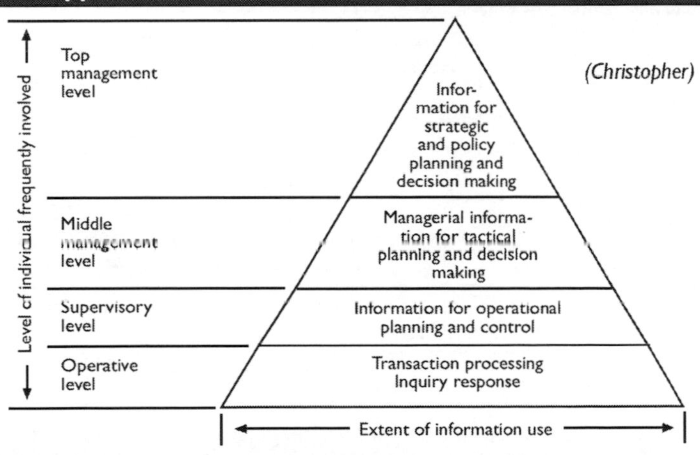

- ☑ Reduced purchase and production cycle times
- ☑ Improved problem-solving and solutions to operational differences/difficulties
- ☑ Improved contract and relationship management
- ☑ Improved inter- and intra-site communications > virtual teams/organisations etc.
- ☑ Improved service, through better knowledge/anticipation of requirements
- ☑ Improved product development (quality, time to market etc)
- ☑ Reduced exposure to risk of supply chain failure, disruption
- ☑ Supplier benefits from reduced selling costs; business security; less likelihood of misunderstood requirements, rejects, disputes; improved capacity planning etc.

4.1 Develop and implement appropriate information and knowledge sharing systems between purchasing departments and suppliers

Development of purchasing information systems

(Minkema; Baily, Farmer & Jessop)

Independence – Purchasing operates to own guidelines > sub-optimisation. Standalone system > operational decisions, computations

↓

Dependence – Dovetailing with other functions via consultation, reporting. Standalone system > operational decisions, data processing

↓

Business integration – Systematic integration with other functions. Integrated system > tactical decisions, efficient order handling, info processing > internal co-ordination (eg supporting MRP)

↓

Chain integration – Systematic co-operation along supply chain. Integrated system > strategic decisions, service focus, management info > internal/external co-ordination (eg supporting JIT)

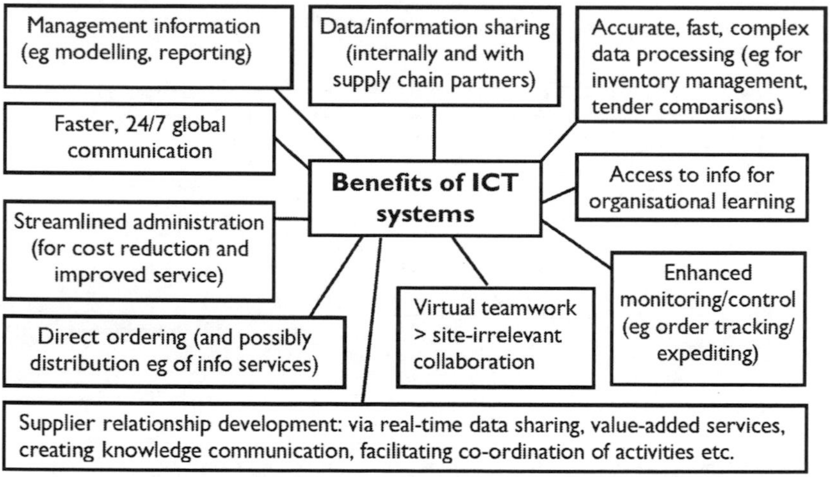

Benefits of ICT systems

- Management information (eg modelling, reporting)
- Data/information sharing (internally and with supply chain partners)
- Accurate, fast, complex data processing (eg for inventory management, tender comparisons)
- Faster, 24/7 global communication
- Access to info for organisational learning
- Streamlined administration (for cost reduction and improved service)
- Enhanced monitoring/control (eg order tracking/ expediting)
- Direct ordering (and possibly distribution eg of info services)
- Virtual teamwork > site-irrelevant collaboration
- Supplier relationship development: via real-time data sharing, value-added services, creating knowledge communication, facilitating co-ordination of activities etc.

Extranet, e-procurement systems >> ***Unit 4.2***

Risks related to info/knowledge-sharing systems

- ❑ Controlling access to intellectual property/capital and confidential data
- ❑ Risk of technology/systems malfunction
- ❑ Contingency risk (viruses, damage)
- ❑ Internal/external risks of hacking, data theft/misuse/corruption, system sabotage etc.
- ❑ Turnover of key personnel, with loss of knowledge and intellectual property

>> Data security controls (passwords, data encryption, access controls)
>> Data protection compliance (Data Protection Act 1998)
>> Preventive maintenance and contingency planning for systems failure/disruption
>> Protection of patents, design rights, copyright, trade marks, confidential information

Analyse the application of technology to automate and streamline key operational processes within the supply chain — 4.2

E-sourcing

E-sourcing is 'using the internet to make decisions and form strategies regarding how and where services or products are obtained' (*CIPS*) ie: purchasing research; requirements definition; tendering; supplier selection; contract award/management. Mainly used by specialist buyers.

E-sourcing tools

- ***Online catalogues.*** Suppliers exhibit products in electronic catalogues, often linked to stock database and e-commerce facilities. Effective catalogues: informative, user-friendly, commerce-enabled (shopping cart, checkout, secure payment).
- ***RFQ/e-tendering,*** using e-RFQs (requests for quotation) and specifications posted online or sent to different suppliers: bids received and evaluated electronically.
- ***E-auctions:*** supplier offers goods and potential buyers bid competitively: highest bid wins. (*Reverse auction:* buyer specifies needs, and suppliers submit competitive quotes)
- ***Market exchanges:*** sites where multiple buyers/sellers meet to exchange goods.
- ***Online supplier evaluation data:*** third-party reports, customer feedback, approved/accredited supplier lists, benchmarking reports, market intelligence tools
- ***Requirement planning/specification tools:*** integrated systems for resource planning (eg ERP), design and development (eg CAD/CAM); trend/spend analysis
- ***Collaborative development forum:*** restricted-access website for exchange of ideas, development plans, best practice.

☑ Access to supplier evaluation and benchmarking information
☑ Overview of sourcing process > better planning, integration
☑ Ready price comparisons (via supplier and third-party sites)
☑ Access to wider supply base (including small, international sources)
☑ Streamlined sourcing: reduced lead times, process efficiencies > cost savings
☑ Standardised approach > best practice development and sharing

E-procurement *[>> Unit 4.3]*

❑ **Automated purchase to pay (P2P) systems:** generate electronic requisitions and purchase/call-off orders; validate suppliers and pricing; automated routing system for budget and management sign-off; invoice generation and matching; processing of paper/electronic payments (eg funds transfer); real-time balance and transaction reporting; electronic archiving.

❑ **Electronic point of sale (EPOS) systems**: feedback data from point of sale terminals (eg using barcodes/RFID scanning). Efficient processing of sales; real-time stock updating and replenishment reports; management info (eg usage rates, sales trends); support for loyalty cards and customer data gathering.

❑ **Electronic funds transfer (EFT) systems**: direct transfer between bank accounts eg EFTPOS (point of sale credit/debit card payment); wage payments; automatic payment transfers to suppliers. Savings in administrative costs; reduction in overall cash cycles within the supply chain (cashflow benefits); improved cash security; automated reconciliation, accounting and management reporting.

4.2 Analyse the application of technology to automate and streamline key operational processes within the supply chain

New technology communication tools

- ❑ Mobile telecommunications (mobile phones, SMS text messaging, m-commerce)
- ❑ Interactive voice-response systems > automated customer service
- ❑ Customer relationship management (CRM) and supplier relationship management (SRM) systems: database linked to integrated transaction processing and contract management functions, sales force automation, integrated computer-telephony systems (for enquiry handling) etc.
- ❑ Virtual meetings technology: video-phones, video-conferencing, web-casting
- ❑ Network- or internet-based information exchange and commerce applications (including e-mail, extranets, e-mail, e-commerce).

Extranet applications

An **extranet** is an intranet (internal network) that is made accessible to selected external partners such as business partners, remote employees, suppliers or key customers, for exchanging data and applications and sharing information. (*Business Link*)

INTERNET *24-7, global, multi-public; data-sharing (online specifications, database access etc) e-commerce (e-sourcing, e-procurement, e-auctions); 'virtual' team/organisation*

EXTRANET *Authorised access to selected publics for data sharing eg with suppliers, customers*

INTRANET *Internal communication: policies, staff info, briefings, database etc*

- ☑ Allows authorised users to access and share data: project/transaction histories, policies, inventory and demand forecast data, contract terms, tender information, release-authorised reports (eg vendor ratings) etc.
- ☑ More flexible, less costly than EDI (dedicated network system).
- ☑ Enables knowledge creation and sharing (without cost of meetings)
- ☑ Integration of communication between dispersed project team members > 'virtual' teamworking, ideas-swapping etc
- ☑ Supports online ordering, order tracking and inventory management > improved supply chain integration
- ☑ Reduced operational costs eg by making manuals, technical docs available online
- ☑ Provides coherent interface (versatile initial touch point)
- ☑ Improved communications security; controlled access to confidential data.

NB: In order to provide tangible value, requires: defined business case; careful planning (scope, levels of access, access/security requirements); user promotion and education.

Automated systems and business risk

- Automated transaction processing, payments, invoice matching, reconciliation etc reduces risk of fraud (eg theft of cash, generating false invoices, payments to false staff/suppliers, inflating/deflating financial results by falsifying stock movements).
- Automated tendering and e-auctions can reduce the risk of corruption (eg buyers receiving bribes or inducements to award contracts on unfair terms)
- Info/knowledge sharing systems can create exposure to loss, theft, corruption or misuse of data/information, loss of intellectual property, breach of confidentiality and disruption to operations due to systems damage or malfunction
- Risk of lost supplier/customer goodwill from misunderstandings, errors, queries etc not handled flexibly or knowledgeable (ie by a human being)!

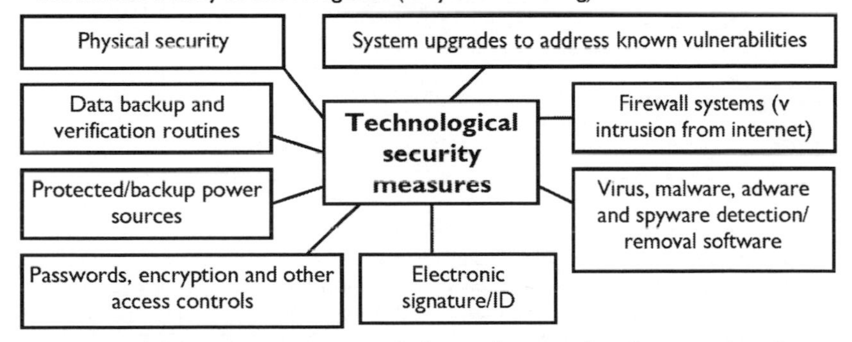

Plus **managerial security measures:** info flow audit, internal audit, segregation of duties, ethics management.

Operational planning and control systems

The syllabus doesn't mention them, but you should also be aware of eg:

Materials requirements planning (MRP): 'a set of logically related procedures, decision rules and records designed to translate a master production schedule (MPS) into time-phased "net requirements" and the planned coverage of such requirements.'

Manufacturing resources planning (MRP II): draws on the MPS to develop materials planning, personnel deployment, maintenance planning and financial analysis (for accurate costing of manufacture).

Enterprise resource planning: consolidates materials, manufacturing, logistics, supply chain, sales/marketing, finance and HR info into one management system >> single database able to offer 'real time' info for solving business problems.

Draw on your studies for *Operations Management in the Supply Chain* for other ideas eg robotics, RFID transport and inventory tracking, automated materials handling and so on.

4.3 Evaluate and explain the benefits of automated processes and info flows and their impact on the supply chain

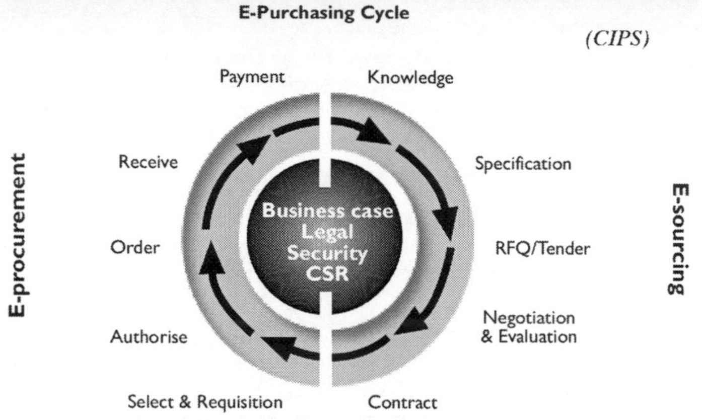

E-procurement is 'using the internet to operate the transactional aspects of requisitioning, authorising, ordering, receipting and payment processes for the required services or products' (*CIPS*) ie: automating 'purchase to pay' cycle. Often used to devolve buying process to local users/business administrators.

- **Automated purchase to pay (P2P) systems:** generate electronic requisitions and purchase/call-off orders; validate suppliers and pricing; automated routing system for budget and management sign-off; invoice generation and matching; processing of paper/electronic payments (eg funds transfer); real-time balance and transaction reporting; electronic archiving.
- ***EDI***: exchange of documents in standardised electronic form, directly from a computer application in one organisation to an application in another. Requires dedicated network (heavy investment): extranets = more flexible/accessible option.
- ***On-line track-and-trace***: global positioning, barcode/RFID > receipt/inspection, inventory management, transport planning, exception 'flagging' for expediting
- ***Electronic point of sale (EPOS) systems***: feedback data from point of sale terminals for inventory control, re-ordering
- ***Contract management systems***: updating e-contracts for changes; reporting by exception on performance discrepancies etc.
- ***Databased information***: storage and managed access > supply market data; customer data; supplier performance data (captured/updated in real time) etc.
- ***E-catalogues, e-tendering and e-auctions*** for e-sourcing.
- **Extranet systems**: selective stakeholder network using ordinary internet links. Allows authorised users (suppliers, partners, customers) to access and share data: project/transaction histories, policies, inventory and demand forecast data, contract terms, tender information, release-authorised reports (eg vendor ratings) etc. Enables knowledge creation and sharing – plus integration of communication between dispersed project team members > 'virtual' teamworking, ideas-swapping etc

Evaluate and explain the benefits of automated processes and info flows and their impact on the supply chain 4.3

Benefits of automated supply chain processes

- ☑ Cost savings: direct costs of tendering, evaluation; better price comparison
- ☑ Improved communication (supporting supplier management and relationships)
- ☑ Fewer errors, higher accuracy, reduced risk of fraud in info processing
- ☑ Reduced cycle/lead times
- ☑ Process efficiencies: reducing time spent on tendering and contract management
- ☑ Compliance (public sector) Efficiency Review and National Procurement Strategy
- ☑ Best practice: encouraging users to adopt best practice and a consistent approach
- ☑ Collaboration: 'virtual buying teams' to increase bargaining power, consolidate orders
- ☑ Real-time info (eg from EOPS/inventory/ordering integration) for management
- ☑ Strategic focus: allowing purchasing professionals to focus on value-added activity
- ☑ E-sourcing > access to wider supply base (including small, international sources) and comparative price/product info

- ☒ Technologies may not be widely adopted within target supply market
- ☒ Preferred suppliers may not be willing/able to use e-purchasing
- ☒ Use of e-auctions/tenders may damage relationships with established suppliers
- ☒ Buying firm may lack skills, infrastructure, info systems, culture for e-purchasing
- ☒ Technological, data security and financial risks must be assessed/managed
- ☒ Ethical implications (fairness, transparency of criteria etc) must be considered
- ☒ Anticipated cost savings may not accrue in practice

[*Limitations/disadvantages not mentioned in the syllabus – but worth being realistic!*]

From the supplier's point of view *(incentive to investment or joint investment)*:

- ☑ Process efficiencies and cost savings in tendering, order processing, invoicing etc
- ☑ Better communication > improved co-ordination, customer service, relationships > revenue stability, forward planning efficiencies, development initiatives
- ☑ Key customers may demand EDI, EPOS replenishment, integrated systems etc.
- ☑ Sales generation, opportunities to tender via online info, web/e-mail marketing etc
- ☑ Fairness and transparency of e-tendering and auctions > ability to compete, competitor data, learning for future bids

- ☒ Systems development costs (incentive for joint investment with buyer)
- ☒ Risk of incompatible systems/protocols (incentive for joint investment with buyer)
- ☒ Over-use of e-auctions: undermines preferred/long-term supplier relationships
- ☒ Loss of business on price criteria (wasted investment in total offering)

NB: data links only add value if *used*! Optimum use of the e-procurement requires:

- Trust (> increasing access to meaningful data, exchange of feedback for improvement)
- Deepening collaboration (> synergies from shared training, systems integration)
- Relationship management (> regular networking, contacts, information exchange)
- Long-term mutual benefit and commitment (to make investment worthwhile)